W9-CPL-177

Tuscany, Umbria and The Marches
32 km/ 20 miles

Mare Adriatico

Ravenna

Cervia

Bellaria

Cesena

Rimini

Riccione

Cattolica

S. Marino

SAN MARINO

Pesaro

Fano

Urbino

Fossombrone

Senigallia

Ancona

S. Maria di Porto Novo

Sirolo

Numana

Ostra

Iesi

Osimo

Recanati

Pergola

Città di Castello

M A R C H E

Cingoli

Gubbio

Fabriano

Macerata

Civitanova Marche

Umbertide

Tolentino

Perugia

Camerino

Fermo

Assisi

Lago Trasimeno

Spello

Amandola

Foligno

S. Benedetto

Marsciano

Porto d' Ascoli

Montefalco

Ascoli Piceno

U M B R I A

Vettore
2478 m

Todi

Norcia

Roseto d. Abruzzi

Spoleto

Arquata

Teramo

Orvieto

Montereale

Pescara

Terni

Penne

Narni

A B R U Z Z I

Viterbo

Rieti

Cittaducale

L'Aquila

Z I O

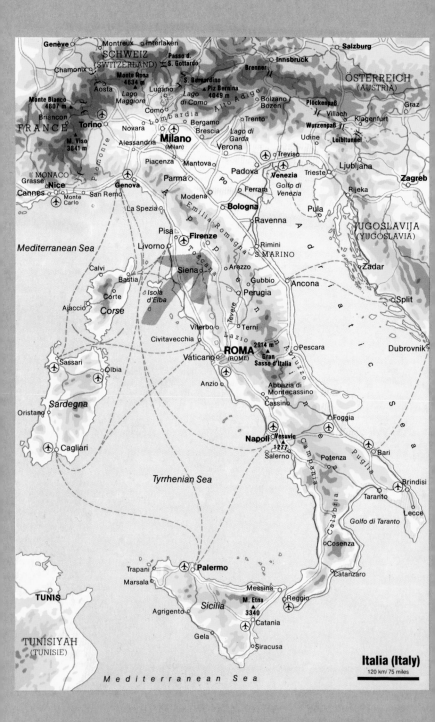

Italia (Italy)

120 km/75 miles

INSIGHT *POCKET* GUIDES

TUSCANY

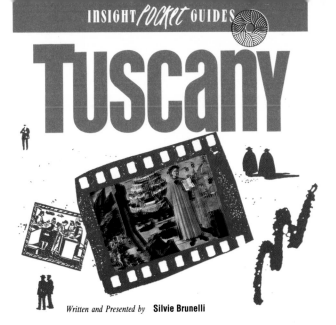

Written and Presented by   **Silvie Brunelli**

INSIGHT
POCKET
GUIDES

Insight Pocket Guide:

Tuscany

Directed by
Hans Höfer

Editorial Director
Andrew Eames

Photography by
Stephano Geraldi
Bill Wassman
Silvia Brunelli

Design Concept by
V. Barl

Design by
Willi Friedrich

© 1993 APA Publications (HK) Ltd

All Rights Reserved

Printed in Singapore by
Höfer Press (Pte) Ltd
Fax: 65-8616438

Distributed in the United States by
Houghton Mifflin Company
2 Park Street
Boston, Massachusetts 02108
ISBN: 0-395-65756-3

Distributed in Canada by
Thomas Allen & Son
390 Steelcase Road East
Markham, Ontario L3R 1G2
ISBN: 0-395-65756-3

Distributed in the UK & Ireland by
GeoCenter International UK Ltd
The Viables Center, Harrow Way
Basingstoke, Hampshire RG22 4BJ
ISBN: 9-62421-518-9

Worldwide distribution enquiries:
Höfer Communications Pte Ltd
38 Joo Koon Road
Singapore 2262
ISBN: 9-62421-518-9

Benvenuto!

Welcome! I was born in Florence and have lived in Tuscany for over 20 years — with a few international interruptions. Now I have my own publishing company here. Introducing my region to visitors, I sometimes mention that locals are inclined to be a mite too boastful about their cultural heritage, or that things don't always work too efficiently. But these are minor inconveniences; all it takes is the scent of wisteria and the view of Florence from the Viale dei Colli with the light of the setting sun warming the city to make me fall in love with Tuscany all over again.

I still find childhood memories a source of inspiration: the chirping of crickets during summer and the taste of *carciofi in pinzimonio*, raw baby artichokes in green olive oil. What a difference from Bonn, where I have also lived! I have returned time and time again to those things that I love.

Foreign visitors have always come here in considerable numbers: from Shelley to Lawrence, Goethe to Stendhal, Tchaikovsky to Dostoyevsky. I'm not surprised: every inch of the ground is steeped in history and sparkles with art. For you, I've tried to pass on the best of my memories in the itineraries in this book, concentrating seven in Florence itself and seven in Tuscany in general. I hope you'll find the latter, which include trips to Pisa, to the castles of Chianti and the caves of Garfagnana, especially enjoyable. I have also provided you with my own selection of restaurants and shops — tried and tested, I assure you! At the back of the book is all the practical information you could possibly need.

We — that is Ilaria, Paola and Simona who assisted me — have tried to show you the various facets of the region: the Tuscany which is a must for all visitors and the other Tuscany which some natives might prefer to keep to themselves — Silvie Brunelli

Contents

Tuscany has always succeeded in preserving its intellectual unity—
even when the region was fragmented or forced to give up its independence. In a sense Tuscany's past is an inseparable part of its
present. Although this does give it dignity, it also constitutes a
burden, with which it is not easy to live.

Florence is about 2,000 years old, but unlike Rome or other
Italian cities it has no mythic origins. Toward the end of the 10th
century BC, the Villanovans settled in the exact spot where the
centre of the city is located today. In the 7th century BC, the
Etruscans settled in the hills surrounding Florence. It is the
Etruscans to whom Tuscany owes its first political institutions and

Palazzo Pitti and Fort Belvedere

Michelangelo's David

the first land utilisation. While remaining a loose association of free cities without becoming a unified state, the Etruscans nevertheless developed a strong sense of solidarity and unity. The Etruscan settlements included Roselle, Vulci, Fiesole, Bolsena, Populonia and Volterra. Within three centuries, however, the Etruscans had been absorbed into new Roman settlements, sometimes forced to do so if they did not join willingly.

During the 1st century BC the Romans founded a colony on the swampy uninviting plain, below Fiesole, giving it the name 'Florentia'. Even today, the centre of Florence is still located on the exact site of that rectangularly designed city, with even the network of streets following those laid out by the Romans. Florentia was a centre of trade. During the 3rd century AD, the city acquired a cosmopolitan character as it attracted merchants and artisans from the East. Christianity was introduced by a Greek named Mynias. Florentia then, under Constantine, became a diocesan town, but the new faith was very slow in spreading.

During the 5th century AD a depression set in which was to last for 500 years. Little is known about the history of the region during the death throes of the Roman Empire. It was, however, ravaged by the Ostrogoths. Even Florence was destroyed and then conquered by the Byzantines and Lombards (from 568 to 774).

None of the Ostrogoths, Byzantines, Lombards or Carolingians, nor even Italy's feudal kings, left substantial traces. Visible evidence of the rediscovery of Roman ideas has been found in the form of

Florence in 1480

the first ring of walls encircling the city—dating to the 6th century and replicating the outline of the original Roman forum.

From the 11th century, Florence grew so fast that the city required a second ring of walls crossing the Arno, making the river an important trade artery. A tremendous flurry of building activity transformed the city into a mediaeval Manhattan with over 150 towers. This was followed by the construction of most of the churches (S Miniato, S Giovanni Battista, S Reparata, SS Apostoli) in Florentine Romanesque style. In the meantime, Florence had won its fight against the local feudal lords and had began battling with neighbouring cities.

The political victory of the bourgeoisie during the 13th century was a result of its economic success. Florentine and Tuscan merchants exported their products to places as far away as London, Bruges and Paris, as well as to the Islamic and Byzantine Orient. In 1252 a gold piece, the florin, was coined—and soon circulated as currency at all the markets of the known world. Up until 1330 Florence remained in the forefront of world trade. Florentines invented numerous elements of today's financial system, including bills of exchange and insurance. Flourishing trade and production drew considerable manpower from the country into the city—following the bourgeois government's abolition of serfdom—while other peasants remained tied to the land around the city through the *mezzadria* system of semi-leasing (whereby landowners split profits with the peasants in return for their labour) which was still being practiced right up to the beginning of this century.

Between 1284 and 1333 a third wall was erected around the city which by now contained 100,000 inhabitants. The name Arnolfo di Cambio—the father of Florentine sculpture—is connected with the rebuilding and transformation of S Reparata into the current cathedral. Another impulse of architectural renewal involved the building of the Palazzo dei Priori (today's Signoria). At the same time Cimabue's work sparked a revival in painting culminating in Giotto's achievements. *Volgare*, the spoken language in Florence acquired literary status and, with the help of Dante's *Divina Commedia*, became the national language.

The proliferation of Gothic architecture during the course of the 14th century contributed a great deal to enhancing the beauty of Tuscan cities. In Florence, for example, a number of buildings were erected, including Santa Croce, Santa Maria del Fiore and Santa Maria Novella. A throng of painters was needed to cover the walls of these churches with frescoes.

Dante Alighieri

Literature flourished: Boccaccio encouraged the development of a culture based on classical writings as well as on the works of Dante and Petrarch. Italian literature was, at the time, equated with Tuscan literature.

In the 14th century, with the plague raging all across Europe bringing medieval civilization to an end, fighting itensified between the *popolo grasso* (literally: the 'fat people'), ie the large merchants and bankers, and the *popolo minuto* (the 'puny people') consisting of craftsmen and small tradesmen. In Tuscany this period of horror was followed by a radical cultural change: the advancement of Humanism through the Renaissance. In 1434 Cosimo de' Medici began to rule the city as a dictator. He did not, however, assume any official offices himself and granted the most powerful families

Detail from Michelangelo's David

not only substantial tax concessions but also the possibility of constraining his rule. Those hostile towards his regime, on the other hand, risked being excluded from business activities and thus faced possible financial ruin. Under the patronage of capitalist groups, which had already come to power in 1382, the Renaissance now began to dawn.

La Primavera by Sandro Botticelli

Whereas the architectural development of the *trecento* (14th century) had centred around the building of churches, the quattrocento saw a shift of focus to palazzi and aristocratic family chapels—led by Brunelleschi's *palazzo* for Luca Pitti and his chapel for the Pazzi family in Santa Croce. It was at this point that Florence consolidated its fame as a city of artists—Beato Angelico (1400–55), Filippo Lippi (1406–69), Luca della Robbia (1400–82), Andrea del Verocchio (1435–88), Antonio del Pollaiolo (1431–98), Domenico Ghirlandaio (1449–94) and Sandro Botticelli (1445–1510), to name only the most important. The best known and most monumental artists, however, were Leonardo da Vinci (1452–1519) and Michelangelo Buonarroti (1475–1564).

Under the rule of the Medici, Neoplatonism became the official state philosophy in Florence, and the Accademia Platonica, founded under Marsilio Ficino, began to convene in Lorenzo de' Medici's villa in Careggi. The Neoplatonists believed in a close connection between philosophical and religious truth, between love and beauty. For a while Lorenzo was able to preserve the political balance in Italy. But the failed attempt of his son and successor, Piero de'Medici, to resist the invading French marked the temporary end of the Medici era. This period was also marked by the steadily growing influence of Girolamo Savonarola, a Dominican monk from Ferrara. Prophesying God's inevitable punishment for Italy's sins, he predicted that from this disaster a new, purified Christianity would emerge. Savonarola was convinced that this radical revival would originate in Florence. An era of austerity began with the official burning of so-called 'vanities'; for example, numerous non-religious paintings by Botticelli were sacrificed to the new ideals. In the end, however, the monk himself was burnt at the stake—which just shows what happens when you get in the way of Florentine business sense and their enjoyment of life.

The appointment to the papacy of two Medici, one shortly after the other, meant an opportunity for their relatives back home, as well as for the monied Florentine bourgeoisie, to make tremendous profits. This practically resulted in a personal union between Rome and Florence. Things went quite well until

Palazzo della Signoria

the year 1527 when the Empire and the Papacy once again locked horns. Florence resisted the attacking imperial army. In 1530 the citizens personally took up arms, with Michelangelo supervizing the planning and construction of fortifications. In the end, however, Florence was forced to surrender.

For the first time since the post-Roman barbarian invasions, Florence fell under foreign rule, and—also for the first time since the plague of 1348—the populace truly suffered. The greatest misfortune, aside from the decline of economic and intellectual activity, was the loss of Republican freedom. This began an era of absolutist rule by papal appointees of Spanish descent, making Florence a kind of Spanish protectorate. Michelangelo left the city. To prevent Florence from being swallowed totally by the Spanish, the 18-year-old Cosimo I, a distant descendant of the Medici, was made Duke. Putting Machiavellian principles into practice, Cosimo restored limited autonomy, as well as stability to the state. It was only after Cosimo brought neighbouring cities under Florentine rule (through a series of brutal battles) that it was possible to

Savonarola being burnt at the stake in Florence

speak of a Tuscan state. Meanwhile, in Rome, Michelangelo became the master to a new generation of artists. Mannerism became the official state art and Giorgio Vasari (1511-74) became not only its most inspired exponent but also the Grand Duchy's 'minister of culture'. This period produced artists such as Bronzino, Benvenuto Cellini, Bartolomeo Ammannati and Bernardo Buontalenti.

Vasari personally undertook changes in Florence's urban development and was responsible for the building of the Uffizi ('offices')—the administration building for the absolutist bureaucracy—along with the Corridoio Vasariano, the connecting passage-way that Vasari built from the Palazzo Vecchio to the seat of the Grand Duke, the Palazzo Pitti.

The 16th century transformed Tuscany, once the cradle of fine art, into a hotbed of scientific activity. Galileo Galilei, the father of modern experimental science, was, however, banished. Then the Thirty Years War robbed Tuscany of its markets. This economic crisis was followed by the plague in 1631. The growing decadence of the Medici contributed to political and economic decline.

At the beginning of the 18th century the Tuscans were able to maintain their autonomy by pushing through their demand that the grand ducal Crown remain separate from the imperial one, thus guaranteeing a Tuscan dynasty. In March of 1799 Tuscany was occupied by Bonaparte's troops. Defeated by the Austrians and the Russians, the French were then forced to withdrew in July of the same year. In 1807, however, Tuscany became part of the French Empire.

The era of the Lorrainers, Ferdinand III and Leopold II, saw Tuscany in a sort of hibernation which served to prevent intervention on the part of the Habsburgs, as well as allowing Florence to survive the crises of 1820–1 and 1831 reasonably unharmed. During the four decades following the Restoration much energy was channeled into building and construction. The façade of the Poggio Imperiale, the interior design of the Palazzo Pitti and the buildings in Via Calzaiuoli are examples of the Classicism of this period. Jean-Pièrre Viesseux started the magazine *L'Antologia*, which soon became the voice of liberal Italian culture. The founding of the University of Pisa gave Tuscany a new institution of learning and created a new point of reference for Italy's intelligentsia.

Santa Croce church

In 1848 the Tuscan army was massacred in the First War of Independence. On 15 March 1860 the announcement of the annexation of Tuscany by Piedmont provided the decisive jolt for the Union of Italy—which was then proclaimed a year later. For tactical political reasons, Florence was made the capital of Italy from 1865–70 before having to relinquish this status to Rome again.

From this point on, Tuscany and the rest of Italy essentially share the same political history. The Second World War took a heavy toll in Florence: bridges, entire streets, historic buildings and paintings were destroyed—and in the year 1966 numerous bridges and works of art fell victim to the heavy floods.

Historical Highlights

BC

700–500 Etruscan civilizations, federation of states.

3rd c The Romans gain power, annex Etruria and found colonies.

27 Emperor Augustus assigns the region of Tuscany (up to the Tiber) to Etruria.

AD

467 Fall of Rome.

493–553 Rule by the Goths.

553–69 Rule by Byzantium.

569 Arrival of the Lombards and creation of the Duchy of Tuscia with its seat in Lucca.

774 After the defeat of the Lombards, the Francs take over Tuscia.

1000–1300 German emperors conquer Italy. Constant fighting between rival parties, the Guelphs and Ghibellines.

1118 Consecration of the cathedral in Pisa.

11th–12th c Romanesque architecture (exemplified by the Cathedral of Pisa).

13th–14th c Gothic architecture: the Cathedral, Santa Maria Novella, Santa Croce and Loggia dei Lanzi in Florence and the Palazzo Publico in Siena.

1348 The plague rages in Florence.

1384 Arezzo is captured by the Florentines.

1406 Pisa is defeated and becomes part of the Florentine state.

1434–64 Cosimo de'Medici, the great art patron, rules Florence.

1469–92 Lorenzo de'Medici, known as 'the Magnificent' rules Florence.

1498 Savonarola is strangled and burned as a heretic.

1555 Florence defeats and annexes Siena.

1564–1642 Galileo Galilei: revolutionary discoveries in the field of physics.

17th–18th c Baroque period.

1743 The House of Medici dies out. The Grand Duchy of Tuscany passes to the House of Lorraine.

1796 Tuscany is occupied by Napoleon's troops.

1808 Annexation of Tuscany by the French Empire.

1815 The Grand Duchy is annexed by the Austro-Hungarian Monarchy.

1848 War of Independence.

1859 Union of Italy.

1865–70 Florence is the capital city of Italy.

1870 Rome is made the capital city of Italy.

1915 Italy enters the First World War on the side of the Allies.

1922 Mussolini is made prime minister by Victor Emmanuel.

1940 Treaty with Germany and Japan; Italy enters the Second World War.

1943 Overthrow of the Fascists.

1943–5 Severe war damage; in Florence all the bridges but the Ponte Vecchio are destroyed.

1945 Execution of Mussolini.

1946 Italy becomes a republic.

1957 Treaty of Rome; Italy is a founder member of the EC.

1966 The Arno floods its banks devastating several sections of Florence and destroying irreplacable works of art and many collections.

1987 'Sorprasso'—the Italian economy overtakes that of the British and French.

1988 Florentines vote for measures to exclude traffic and control pollution.

FLORENCE

TOUR ①

Art in Concentrated Form

Cathedral and Baptistry; in Giotto's tower; down Via Calzaiuoli past Orsanmichele, Piazza della Signoria with the Palazzo Vecchio and Loggia dei Lanzi; Ponte Vecchio.

The buildings and places listed above make up the heart of the old city containing the majority of monuments. Here you will also find the best—and unfortunately the most expensive—shops in Florence, as well as restaurants, bars and a great deal more. Nobody lives here any more, especially not since sections of the quarter were made traffic-free zones—the palazzi house almost nothing but offices.

So let us turn our attention to the historic quarter, the *Centro Storico*, as well as to the business section—art and history on the one hand, fashion and pizza *al taglio* (off the baking tray) on the other. These streets offer the *summa* of Florentine art and culture. Our starting point is at the **Piazza del Duomo**. The construction of the Cathedral of Florence—properly called **S Maria**

Statues in front of the Palazzo Vecchio

The Cathedral and Palazzo Vecchio

del Fiore—was actually begun under the supervision of Arnolfo di Cambio during the last years of the 13th century. Brunelleschi, however, was the most important architect: it was he who succeeded in erecting the dome—at that time an almost impossible feat. The current façade was not added until 1888—construction continued on the cathedral, in other words, for six centuries.

In the mid-16th century Doni wrote that he was convinced that by sitting on the steps outside the cathedral you could hear any language. Standing outside the cathedral today it looks as if that statement remains true. Except on rainy days you will see tourists sitting there from the four corners of the world: eating ice cream, sunning themselves, writing postcards or feeding the pigeons.

The interior of the **Cathedral** is impressive due to the austerity of its architectural lines—providing one can even see them: the numerous scaffolds usually prevent you from getting an overall impression and a proper sense of space. By climbing the 463 steps, you can reach the dome and look at the Vasari frescoes (from 10am–5pm, admission: 4,000 lire). The cathedral windows—mostly by Ghiberti, who also created the Paradise Portals of the Baptistry—are remarkable, as are the statues of the prophet Daniel, attributed to Donatello, and the Giotto monument.

Steps lead down to **S. Reparata** in the crypt (open from 10am–5pm, admission fee

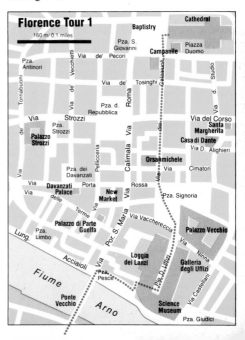

The Cathedral Dome

2,000 lire), the precursor of the current cathedral going back to the 5th or 6th century. If you are in good shape you should definitely climb to the top of the **Campanile** (from 8:30am–7:30pm, admission: 4,000 lire)—the view is ample compensation for tired feet. Giotto actually intended to build it almost 130ft (40m) higher. Only managing to complete the first storey, however, he had to leave its completion to his successors. On display on the first and second floors you will find ornamentation by Donatello and Pisano—works, for example, such as *The Planets*, *The Virtues* and *The Sacraments*. The steep staircase gets narrower the higher you climb. The window slits along the stairs provide a small glimpse of what awaits you at your destination. The view from the top is like having the most important buildings in Florence presented to you on a tray—making you realize how small the historic heart of Florence really is. See how compact everything is, clustered together, encircled by the usually green Tuscany hills. The red roofs below, fanning out in all directions, are an extraordinary sight which lets you forget the grey tones of concrete that lie beneath some of them. Directly next to us the dome arches upward more mightily than ever.

Back on the ground it is time for a breather: let us spend it in

The Cathedral

the **Gran Caffé** right next to the Baptistry. Here you can enjoy the typically Florentine synergy of artistic sensibility and business sense: the bar is heavily patronised because of its frescoes, probably by a Sienese master.

Having refreshed body and soul we are ready to take on the **Paradise Portals** of the Baptistry, three large doors with bronze inlay work, mainly fashioned by Ghiberti. These are, in fact, recently mounted copies—the originals were so damaged by air

Orsanmichele

pollution that they were moved to the Museo dell'Opera del Duomo. The north and east doors are particularly significant.

The **Baptistry** was erected in the 11th century on the site of a Lombardic or even Early Christian building (which is why it was long assumed to be a Roman temple). Up until the 19th century the Baptistry was the only baptismal chapel in Florence. An unusual method was used to count those awaiting baptism: beans were placed for each child in a bowl by the door—a dark bean meant a little boy, a light one a little girl. Dante, amongst others, was baptized here. Inside you will find frescoes of *The Last Judgement*, the work of a 13th century Venetian master on which the young Giotto may have collaborated.

In the **Loggia del Bigallo**, or rather in the museum in this building—at the corner of **Via Calzaiuoli** (Cobbler's Alley)—you will find a fresco dated 1342 showing the oldest surviving view of Florence. Via Calzaiuoli is one of the main shopping streets—and the prices are accordingly high. How about trying an ice cream on Via de Tavolini, the second street on the left? **Perche no?** ('Why not?') is one of the best ice cream parlours in Florence. Personally, I prefer to have a glass of red wine at the Viviano on **Via dei Cimatori**. There used to be plenty of these little wine bars where you could just have a sip of wine in passing—for the Tuscans like to see to it that their blood alcohol level does not drop too low. Note also the shop next door where advertizing signs are made.

Across the street is the **Orsanmichele** church—the name being a contraction of *Ortii* (garden) *di San Michele*. This strange building used to double as a granary and an oratory. The lower floor was an open-columned hall where hawkers could seek shelter from the sun and rain. In Florence commerce and prayer have always been inseparable. Later the building also became the seat of the guilds. The statues in the exterior niches are predominantly by Ghiberti. To the right you will find the **Palazzo del'Arte della Lana** or 'wool guild palace' consisting of three buildings dating from the 13th century and connected with Orsanmichele

Palazzo Vecchio and the Uffizi

by an aerial corridor. The ground floor is occupied by Zanobetti, one of the most tasteful clothing stores in Florence. If you like, you can make a small detour to the beautiful **Palagio di Parte Guelfa**, once the seat of the Guelf Captains.

The next stop is the **Mercato Nuovo**, an open-columned hall in which everything is sold, from flowers to embroidered tablecloths. The buyers are mostly tourists, naturally—who can improve their chances of returning to Florence by patting the nose of the bronze *Porcellino* (a sort of wild pig) sitting out front. Then we follow **Via Vacchereccia** to **Piazza della Signoria** (not Signor*ina*, as many foreigners say!). Outside the **Palazzo Vecchio** there are several statues—the best-known being the omnipresent *David* (a copy; the original is in the Museum of the Academy of Fine Arts/Accademia delle Belle Arti, 60 Via Ricasoli). Donatello's *Judith* (also a copy) stands next to him. The original is inside, in the Sala delle Udienze. *Judith* and *David* are embodiments of the Republican idea of freedom, for Judith liberated her people from the tyranny of Holophernes and David rescued his land from the threat of the giant, Goliath.

The *Neptune* fountain, which the Florentines call *Biancone* ('White Giant'), was installed in honour of the wedding of Francesco de'Medici and Joanna of Austria. Just before you reach it, look for a sign on the ground marking the spot where the Dominican monk Savonarola was burnt at the stake.

The inner courtyard of the Palazzo Vecchio is noteworthy for its painted views of the free cities of the old German Empire—an additional hommage to the Habsburg bride; the rooms inside, such as the Salone de Cinquecento and, on the second floor, the Quartieri Monumentali ('Sumptuous Rooms') offer additional at-

The Uffizi across the Arno

tractions (open from 9am–7pm; Sunday and Friday from 8am–1pm, closed on Saturday; there is also an entrance for the handicapped). The municipal authority is located at the back of the Palazzo Vecchio which is why you may meet a wedding couple or two here.

Piazza della Signoria

Back outside you have the **Uffizi** where you may want to spend the rest of the afternoon, and where you can make your way to the terrace café located on top of the **Loggia de Lanzi** (reached through the west corridor of the gallery). On returning to the Piazza della Signoria, you can inspect the Loggia from ground level. Opened in 1381, the Loggia was once the meeting place of the municipal government. The most important statues sheltering here are Cellini's *Perseus* and the *Rape of the Sabines* by Giambologna. By now you have deserved a treat. Sitting in the sun drinking a cup of coffee outside the **Rivoire** is pure enjoyment.

If you still feel like walking, go down **Por Santa Maria** to the **Ponte Vecchio**, the oldest bridge in Florence. As early as the 13th century craftsmen had set up shop on the bridge. Only jewellers and goldsmiths were allowed to do business here because anything else would have been too 'dirty' in the eyes of the Grand Duke Ferdinand I. **Corridoio Vasariano**, the aerial corridor connecting the Palazzo Vecchio and the Palazzo Pitti crosses this bridge. Here the prices range from 10,000 to 100,000,000 lire—what you buy depends on how full your wallet is. If you don't want to shop, just enjoy the views from the bridge and the stream of passers-by.

The Silver Arno

Piazza Santa Maria Novella with its churches; along the Arno; Via Tornabuoni, Florence most elegant street; Palazzo Strozzi.

Only recently has **Piazza S. Maria Novella** become fully enjoyable: before they blocked off the traffic it was the scene of the city's worst traffic jams with the usual honking and suffocating fumes. Today you can sit on a bench and take in the serenity and regularity of the church façade designed by Leon Battista Alberti—completely forgetting the modern world of the train station behind it.

The Dominican church of **Santa Maria Novella** was completed in 1300 with financial support from the Florentine merchant Giovanni Rucellai. Not surprisingly, in this city saturated with history, this building, too, had a predecessor: the church of Santa Maria della Vigna (Holy Mary of the Vineyard) was surrounded by vineyards and went back to the year 1064. Inside, the frescoes by Ghirlandaio with his self-portrait are a must, as well as works by Masaccio (*The Trinity*) and Giotto (a crucifix) (open Monday–Saturday from 7:15–11:30am and 3:30–5pm).

To the right of the church in the **Chiostro Verde** there are works by Paolo Uccello. The church also offers interesting frescoes in the **Cappellone degli Spagnoli**, the former chapter hall, which in 1556 was placed at the disposal of the Spanish community in Florence (open Monday–Saturday from 9am–2 pm, Sunday from 8am–1 pm, closed on Friday). One of the frescoes includes some black-and-white dogs—an allegorical reference to the Dominicans (*domini canes*), the 'Dogs of Our Lord'. 'Purified' and strengthened we head to the right off Piazza Santa Maria Novella into **Via della Scalla**. Even if you do not intend to buy anything (I highly recommend the soaps and creams, as well as the

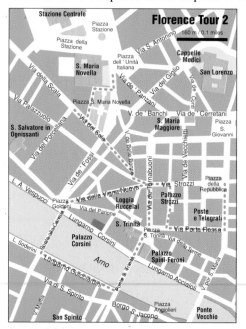

Santa Maria Novella

Dominican-brewed liqueur), you should definitely peek inside the old pharmacy at No. 16. Otherwise, pop across the street to the **Café Voltaire**; in the evenings jazz concerts and other performances are often held here.

After this refreshing stop we continue down Via della Scala and **Via della Vigna Nuova** with their elegant shops and splendid palazzi (the Palazzo Rucellai houses the Alinari photography museum) to the **Ponte alla Carraia**, the second oldest bridge in the city. It has been standing since 1218; the current version, however, goes back to 1559. From here you can see the **Ponte Santa Trinita**, the oldest bridge (erected in 1257, washed away and rebuilt, destroyed by the Germans in 1945 and reconstructed in 1957) and of course the **Ponte Vecchio**. The view is well worth a photograph.

Unfortunately it is a long time since the waters of the Arno were silver—as described in the famous song, *Arno d'argento*—and a bit more greenery along the paved shores would also be nice—but no, we might as well accept the fact: Florence *is* a city of stone—with even its gardens hidden and accessible only from within the buildings.

Our route now takes us across the bridge and along **Lungarno Guicciardini** (note the magnificent palazzi on

Lazing by the Arno

Ponte Vecchio

the right and left banks of the Arno, especially the Palazzo Corsini on the opposite bank with its famous private collection) to the **Ponte Santa Trinita** (if you are particularly in a hurry, you can stay on the same side of the river and walk along Lungarno Corsini). From here, cross the bridge into **Via de'Tornabuoni**, the most elegant shopping street in Florence. The corner, at **Lungarno Acciaiuoli**, is dominated by the mighty **Palazzo Spini Feroni**, one of the largest medieval palazzi, whose construction was begun in 1289. Today it is the seat of the famous shoe company Ferragamo—Florence was and will remain the city of merchants.

On **Piazza Santa Trinita** there is the church of the same name going back to the 14th century (the previous building on the same site existed as early as 1077); the façade was finished in 1593. The interior still bears characteristic Gothic elements. Like so many churches it contains chapels commissioned and decorated by wealthy merchant families hoping to ensure their souls'

salvation—the most important being the **Cappella Sassetti** with its Ghirlandaio frescoes. The main wall bears a representation of Piazza della Signoria with the Palazzo Vecchio and the Loggia dei Lanzi, while on the right we see the donor, Francesco Sassetti, between his son and his friend Lorenzo de' Medici. This is the most important contemporary portrait of Lorenzo. The fresco *Miracle of the Resurrected*

Boy portrays Santa Trinita with its former Romanesque façade and Palazzo Spini where the careless boy had fallen out of a window.

A *panino tartufato*, truffle sandwich at **Procacci** (64r Via Tornabuoni, on the right side of the street) accompanied by a glass of red wine—that is always a pleasure which we would not like to do without in this somewhat dusty city. If, however, this has only whetted your appetite and you are still feeling hungry, then I recommend you walk further down **Via Tornabuoni** to the **Cantinetta Antinori** (3 Piazza Antinori). My personal tip: *crostini all toscana* and *pappa al pomodoro* with a good glass of *Sassicaia or Antinori brut* (it will not be cheap; get your credit card ready).

The **Palazzo Antinori** is one of the few buildings in Florence continuously owned by one and the same family—since 1506. **San Gaetano**, the baroque-like church across the street was mentioned as early as the 11th century.

We now return to **Via Strozzi** and to the **Palazzo Strozzi**. Its size, (like that of the Palazzo Rucellai) demonstrates how keen the owner was on erecting a monument to himself. Filippo Strozzi had astrologers calculate precisely the most favourable time during the year 1489 for the laying of the foundation stone. To build this 'detached family house' so that two façades would be visible simultaneously from a number of different perspectives, Filippo Strozzi had 15 buildings torn down. In those days apparently nobody cared about humane urban development. Today changing exhibitions and the famous antique fair, *Mostra dell'Antiquariato*, are held in the Palazzo.

So we have seen what a Florentine house looks like from the outside, but what is it like to live in one? The forerunner of all palazzi, the **Palazzo Davanzati** houses the **Museo della Casa Fiorentina Antica** with its well-furnished

Piazza della Repubblica

rooms dating from the 15th century (Piazza Davanzati; open from 9am–2pm; holidays from 9am–1pm).

Had enough of Renaissance, of churches and museums for today? Why not treat yourself to an aperitif at **Gilli**'s on **Piazza della Repubblica** (note the interior decoration), the playground for all those who wish to be seen. *Salute*!

Gothic Florence

Badia; Bargello; Santa Croce; then to the flea market.

The area around **Badia** (Via del Proconsolo) and **Bargello** (Via del Proconsolo/corner of Via Ghibellina) makes up the centre of medieval Florence. The **Badia** (abbey) was the church of the wealthiest monastery in the medieval city—founded by Benedictines in the 10th century. The first pre-Romanesque building is no longer standing and all that remains of the second building begun in 1285 is a portion of the apse. In 1627 the church was restructured to give it its present appearance. Inside you will discover Filippo Lippi's *Apparizione della Vergine a S Bernardo* (The Holy Virgin appearing before St Bernhard) and the Chiostro degli Aranci (open from 9–11.45am, 4.30–6pm).

The Bargello (Old Italian for 'the thug'), the oldest palazzo surviving from the communal period (1254–61) was both a fortified prison and the seat of the mayor. Today the massive building with the beautiful courtyard—where from 1502–1782 death sentences were carried out—houses the National Museum with the most significant works of Florentine sculpture (works by Michelangelo, Giambologna, Donatello, Verrocchio; open Monday–Saturday from 9am–2pm, Sunday 9am to 1pm; admission: 3,000 lire).

Heading along the **Via dell'Anguillara**, one of the oldest streets

Florence Tour 3

160 m / 0.1 miles

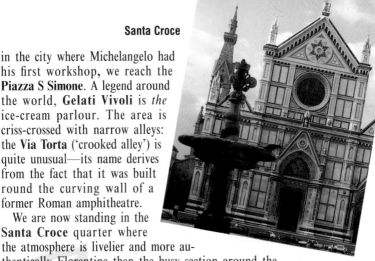

in the city where Michelangelo had his first workshop, we reach the **Piazza S Simone**. A legend around the world, **Gelati Vivoli** is *the* ice-cream parlour. The area is criss-crossed with narrow alleys: the **Via Torta** ('crooked alley') is quite unusual—its name derives from the fact that it was built round the curving wall of a former Roman amphitheatre.

We are now standing in the **Santa Croce** quarter where the atmosphere is livelier and more authentically Florentine than the busy section around the cathedral. A characteristic corner of this quarter is the **Piazza S Pier Maggiore**—jokingly called the 'Piazza S Pierino' (little Peter) because the square is so tiny. Here the shops are not as elegant or as expensive, and not as dependent upon tourism, as those in the centre. Here you will find small vegetable stores and craftsmen. There are also genuine Florentines living in the houses and buildings!

The large, square **Piazza Santa Croce**—the site of the annual historical *Calcio in Costume*, a football game played in Renaissance clothing—is surrounded by 15th and 16th century palazzi (pay special attention to the Palazzo Cocchi Serristori and, opposite it, the Palazzo dell'Antella, south side, Nos 21–22). The Gothic **Santa Croce Church** (what a difference from Northern European Gothic!) was erected by Franciscans—as far away as possible from their rivals, the Dominicans of S Marco—in 1226, shortly after the death of St Francis of Assisi (open from 8am–12.30pm, 3pm–6.30pm). The building was completed in 1380; the façade, like that of the Cathedral, dates from the 19th century.

The interior is dominated by Florentine austerity and Franciscan simplicity combined with the large spaciousness of Early Christian basilicas; the chapels of the Bardi and Peruzzi families—a family chapel in Santa Croce was *the* status symbol in Trecento Florence—has frescoes by Giotto and members of his workshop that are particularly worth seeing. Another privilege enjoyed by very few was to be buried here, in the Florentine Pantheon: Michelangelo, Galileo and Machiavelli, all found their last peace here. The empty sarcophagus next to Michelangelo's gravestone is particularly noteworthy: this is where Dante, first banished from Florence and then asked to return, was meant to lie. But the city of Ravenna, where the poet died, never returned his remains.

You have to leave the church in order to look around the **Pazzi Chapel**, the former chapter house. Attributed to Brunelleschi, this Early Renaissance building (1430) creates an impressive contrast to the Gothic church; in the **Museo dell'Opera di Santa Croce** a crucifix by Cimabue is a particular eye-catcher.

The **Via delle Pinzochere** will take you to **Casa Buonarroti** (Via Ghibellina 70) which once belonged to Michelangelo, though he never lived here. The museum in the house has two of Michelangelo's early works. Following **Borgo Allegri**, the street in Florence with the worst reputation, we arrive at the **Piazza dei Ciompi**, where you can rummage around at the flea market.

Heading to the right into the **Via Pietrapiana** and across the **Piazza S Ambrogio** (with a 15th–16th-century church) will take you to the food market on the **Piazza Ghiberti**. The **Cibreo** (also known as 'Caffe Cibreo' or 'Cibreo Alimentari'), is excellent but not cheap and is equally suitable as a place to stop for an aperitif or a snack, for lunch or dinner (Via de' Macci 118r).

Oltrarno

The Palazzo Pitti Museum in the morning; after relaxing in the Boboli Gardens a walk through the characteristic San Frediano quarter with its Santo Spirito, Carmine and Cestello churches.

To get off to a good start, we will have breakfast in the **Caffe** at 9 Piazza Pitti. **Piazza Pitti** would make a quite different impression if it weren't for the miserable parking lot—but underground and multi-storey carparks are simply considered inappropriate for a historical city like Florence. The Palazzo was built for the wealthy merchant Luca Pitti in 1457 and in 1549 was bought

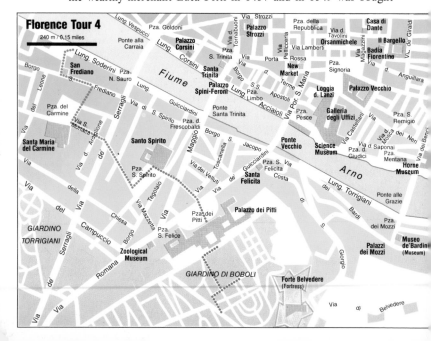

Ice cream in the Piazza Pitti

and extended by Eleonora of Toledo, the wife of Cosimo I. The building then remained the royal seat of the Grand Dukes of Tuscany for three centuries. During the time of Napoleon, Bonaparte's sister, the Queen of Etruria, lived here. Until 1949 the Palazzo was the residence of members of the House of Savoy.

Although it has not been clearly determined who the architect of this huge building was, Brunelleschi may have provided the blueprints. Inside we find the **Galleria Palatina** containing the private collection of the Grand Dukes of Tuscany (opening times for all the museums in the Palazzo Pitti: 9am–2pm; holidays 9am–1pm; closed Monday). The works displayed range from Renaissance to Baroque with highlights by Raphael and Titian, as well as by Rubens and Van Dyck. The **Galleria d'Arte Moderna** offers mainly 19th century painting. Works by the Tuscan *Macchiaioli*, late 19th-century Impressionists whose number included Giovanni Fattori, Telemaco Signorini and Giovanni Boldini, are particularly interesting. The **Museo degli Argenti** with its items of worked gold and silver, ivory carvings and other objects is also worth visiting.

If we are in luck and the sun is shining, I would recommend a walk around the **Boboli Gardens**, a prime example of gardening *all'italiana*. The prettiest part is the southern portion nearest the Porta Romana. The garden is decorated with hundreds of marble statues—one of the best-known being the Fontano di Bacco, the Bacchus Fountain. The rider on the tortoise was actually the court dwarf of Cosimo I.

Other features of the garden include the building that even the Italians call by the

Santo Spirito

German name **Kaffeehaus**, since it was built for the Austrian nobleman, Peter Leopold of Habsburg-Lorraine. Then there is the neoclassical building, La Meridiana, that contains the **Museo del Costume** with its gowns and costumes of eras gone by. The Grand Dukes raised silkworms in the Giardino del Cavaliere and this is where the first potato from America was planted in Italy.

Back outside we cross the Piazza Pitti and continue straight ahead into the alley called **Scrucciolo dei Pitti** (literally: 'Pitti Slide'). Next we encounter the **Via Maggio**, once intended as the triumphant approach to Manneristic Florence, running from the Porta Romana across Santa Trinita Bridge and along the Via Tornabuoni. Today Via Maggio is the antique dealers' street. At No 26, Via Maggio we discover the house built by Buontalenti from 1570–74 for Bianca Cappello—first the mistress, then the wife of Ferdinando de'Medici; it is a fine example of the decorated palazzi of the end of the Cinquecento.

We now arrive in the **San Frediano** quarter where you will encounter few tourists, even in the high season, and where the traditional Florentine lifestyle still thrives. This is evident in the numerous workshops and the crowds of people in the street—the atmosphere being one of bustling activity, not of stress and strain. Next we reach the **Piazza Santo Spirito** with, on your right, the church of the same name (built by Brunelleschi from 1434–82) with its elegant, unfinished façade.

The Augustinians who had the first building erected here in the 13th century also provided quarters for itinerants, a hospital for the sick and a kitchen for the needy. Later their monastery became a centre of humanistic education: Boccaccio left them his library. The legend has it that for decades the monks did without one meal a day to finance the new elaborate building created by Brunelleschi.

As with so many of his projects, Brunelleschi did not live to see this building completed. The basic design of the building is that of a hall church (basilica) with a central ground plan. All of the elements of the building are carefully interrelated. Unfortunately the intended overall effect is disturbed by elements added later, such as the Baroque baldachino over the altar. Better by far, in the Cenacolo di Santo Spirito, is a *Crucifixion* fesco from the original monastery. The square outside (note the palazzo on the corner of Via Mazzetta, built in 1503 for the wealthy silk merchant Rinieri Dei) was the meeting place for the 'in' crowd in the Seventies with the **Bar Ricchi** as its focal point (perhaps you would like to take a seat in the sun for a glass of *prosecco*). In the Eighties, on the other hand, the local scene converged on the nearby **Plazza del Carmine** (follow Via S Agostino and Via Santa Monaca to get there). But the atmosphere is totally different: **dolce vita** is the scenario for today's hedonism.

Here, too, you will find an important church: **Santa Maria del Carmine**. Begun for the Carmelite Order in 1268, the original Florentine Gothic building was destroyed by a fire in 1771. Fortu-

In the Boboli Gardens

nately the famous **Brancacci Chapel** with its revolutionary Masaccio frescoes were saved. Having begun the chapel's frescoes around 1424, Masolino left Florence for an appointment as court painter in Budapest. Masaccio, his friend and eighteen years his junior, took over until Masolino's return—after which the two painters completed significant portions together. After both died Filippo Lippi completed the cycle in 1485.

It is not easy to distinguish the work of the three different painters—Masolino still used the soft lines of international Gothic, whereas Masaccio is much more dramatic and expressive. Another characteristic feature of Masaccio's style is the use of specific light sources. In the upper right of the middle field, in the fresco representing Peter in the act of healing, Masaccio renders a clear picture of the Florence of his time.

Crossing **Borgo San Frediano** we approach a true gem, the small Baroque church of **San Frediano in Castello** whose dome provides an important accent within the panorama of the city. If you have deleveloped an appetite we can stop in at **Angiolino** (36, Via Santo Spirito); for a snack try **Cantinone del Gallo Nero** (6r, Via Santo Spirito) where you can also quench your thirst, particularly for wine.

Tracking Down the Medici

Culture and then lively market chaos: the clothing market and the food market; followed by lunch.

Piazza SS Annunziata ('SS' stands for *Santissima*—exceptionally holy) is near the university (Piazza Brunelleschi). Coming from the west it actually marks the beginning of the city centre. The *loggia* (arcade) of the **Spedale degli Innocenti**, built by Brunelleschi around 1420 and containing *tondi* (roundels) by Luca della Robbia, was copied on the opposite side a century later by Antonio da Sangall. The unity which this gave to the piazza was so pleasing that the loggia was extended in front of the church, creating an ensemble which emanates a strong sense of calm. Looking across the street you will see the **Palazzo Budini Gattai** on the right, today the seat of the Tuscan state government, and on the left the hotel, Loggiato de Serviti, with its antique furnishings. The statue of **Ferdinando de'Medici** which dominates the square is modelled after the statue of Marcus Aurelius in the Campidoglio in Rome.

The portico of SS **Annunziata**, also known as the *Chiostrino dei Vati*, contains frescoes by Andrea del Sarto, who also created the *Madonna del Sacco* and the *Madonna de Morti* inside. Numerous 16th century artists (eg Leon Battista Alberti) are buried within this church.

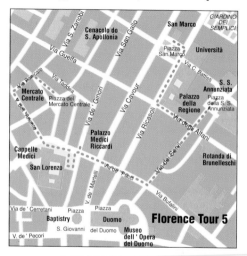

Florence Tour 5

San Lorenzo

In the **Galleria dello Spedale** degli Innocenti the *Madonna e Angelo* by Botticelli and the *Epifania* by Ghirlandaio (open Monday, Tuesday, Thursday and Saturday 9am–7pm; admission: 2,000 lire) are especially worth mentioning. A large portion of the Medici collection of ancient art is housed in the **Museo Archeologico**, including the Etruscan Statues *Chimera*, *Idolino* and *The Actor* (36 Via della Colonna; open Tuesday–Saturday 9am–2pm; Sunday 9am–1pm).

The next stop is practically a must: **San Marco** monastery, on the piazza of the same name, is reached by heading left down Via Battisti. Taking in the gentle frescoes by Beato Angelico in the modest cells where the austere monk, Savonarola, once lived, you may wind up asking yourself why our way of living requires so many material things. In Florence, fortunately, all the interesting sights are close together, so while you are searching for that answer you can wander the short walk down to the **Accademia** (careful: the emphasis is on the 'e') **delle Belle Arti** in **Via Ricasoli**. Here the real *David* self-confidently 'holds his own', but hardly manages to steal the show from the unfinished *Prigioni* (also by Michelangelo). A few years ago a well-known company gave a PR banquet right here at the foot of *David*; postcards and T-shirts offer further examples of the kind of abuse which poor David has to put up with.

How about a breather—a glass of wine perhaps at **Fani**'s on the corner of **Via degli Alfani** and **Via de Serfi**? Or, if you prefer, a *cappuccino* on **Piazza San Marco** at the bar of the same name. Then continue down **Via Cavour** to **Fetrinelli** bookstore, meeting place of Florentine students and intellectuals (they also have a good stock of foreign-language books). Looking across the street you will see the **Palazzo Medici Riccardi**. Originally intended as the town residence of the Medici, the building also housed the administrative offices of the family bank as well as the commercial headquarters. If you want to take a look inside, the **Cappella del Palazzo** is worth your time for the Flemish-Master-like frescoes by Benozzo Gozzoli, painted in the style of the Flemish Masters from the years 1452 to 1460. The frescoes include portraits of several members of the Medici family. The frescoes in the **Luca Giordano Room**, on the other hand, are a veritable apotheosis of the Medici (open 9am–5pm., holidays from 9–12am, closed on Wednesday).

Returning to the street, turn immediately right into Via de' Gori. Practically hidden behind the sales carts, the *barroccini*, you will find **S Lorenzo Church**—the first truly Renaissance church. It was built by Filippo Brunelleschi from 1421–69, although its origin goes back to Early Christian times (it is one of the oldest churches in Florence).

In 1418 when construction work began to expand the church, an entire neighbourhood was torn down to make room. Soon, however, work had to be halted, since the long-running war against the neighbouring town of Lucca had drained the city treasury. Thus it was that Cosimo de'Medici offered to finance the remaining work. This is how S Lorenzo became the family church of the Medici. Only the façade remains unfinished—since nobody could agree on the design. Today Florentines say that the façade is more beautiful as it is, besides fitting the rustic Palazzo Medici better this way. Of particular interest inside, you will find the *Sacrestia Vecchia*, a tabernacle by Desiderio di Settignano, sculptures by Donatello and a reredos by Filippo Lippi.

Next to the church (to your left when you are facing the main portal) there is also a **library** bearing the name 'Medici'—having been erected on behalf of Pope Clement VII (one of Lorenzo's brothers; open Monday–Saturday 9am–1pm; admission is free). This room by Michelangelo represents a prime example of the Mannerist style in Renaissance architecture. In 1990 there were veritable street battles outside the church between the *ambulanti*, the owners of the street carts, and the police who attempted to enforce an ordinance passed by the city administration banishing street traders. Quite in keeping with the Biblical example, the police sought to banish the merchants from the steps of the church. The police failed, and it is not just tourists who shop here, at the **mercantino**: Florentines do so as well since the prices are quite low. Bargaining, however, is no longer the usual thing—at the most you might be able to bargain the price down 1,000 or 2,000 lire. You will find all types of clothing on display here, as well as leather goods, tablecloths, shoes and plenty of other things.

We now proceed through the market and around the church (there are good views of beautiful roof gardens on the various

palazzi) until we reach **Piazza della Madonna degli Aldobrandini** on our left. There we find the **Cappella dei Medici**, conceived as a magnificent mausoleum. The atmosphere inside the marble **Cappella dei Principi** is oppressive and gloomy, a rare example of Baroque architectural style in Florence. What a contrast: the **Sacrestia Nuova** (1524) contains the famous sculptures by Michelangelo (Lorenzo, the brooder, between *Dawn* (feminine) and *Dusk* (masculine); Giuliano, the man of action, between *Day* and *Night*). Malicious Florentines say that the female figures look rather unfeminine, claiming that Michelangelo (being homosexual) never set eyes on a naked woman in his entire life. Art historians, on the other hand, assume that he simply preferred male models.

The **Sacrestia Vecchia** (Brunelleschi) and **Sacrestia Nuova** (Michelangelo) mark the beginning and end of the Renaissance: it is astonishing that these two significant works are located in one and the same building, making it possible to view them back-to-back.

By now, it is high time we looked after our physical well-being: on the right, in **Via dell'Ariento** you have the **Casa del Vino** (wine and snack bar) with a guaranteed local Florentine clientele. The more courageous souls among you may try a *panino con la trippa or panino col lampredotto* (tripe or pig's intestine sandwiches) at the cart across from the Pasticceria Sieni. If you have a larger appetite, you can walk across the street to the **Mercato Centrale**, the market hall where you can not only buy meat, fish, vegetables and fruit, but also enjoy Tuscan cooking—with a crash course in authentic Tuscan cursing thrown in.

Behind the market, in **Via Rosina**, there is more genuine Florentine atmosphere in concentrated form waiting for you. Despite the considerable crowd of hungry guests, you hardly ever have to wait long for a seat; equally you will hardly have swallowed your last bite when you will be 'asked' to leave—with typical Florentine friendliness ('You're still stuffing your face?!'). But the place is cheap and the food is good! Should you desire something more noble, however, you will be better off at the restaurant **Taverna del Bronzino** (Via delle Ruote, approximately 10-minute walk), which is more stylish and more expensive.

TOUR 6

Romans and Etruscans

Today we head five miles (8km) to the northwest of Florence, to the town of Fiesole located on top of a hill.

The Walk

Today we climbed the mountain
Which Florentines
Always have in mind
To visit old Fiesole.
In the cloister there we feasted our eyes
On Giotto and on pious John
In the splendour of books.
But finally we climbed higher
Up to the top
Where secluded under cypresses
The Franciscan monastery lies.
A cold wind whistles through the mountains,
After the storm the area is gloomy,
Where the eye wanders afar,
Beyond rocks, down through valleys
And at our feet lie Fiesole and Florence.

Ludwig Tieck

Fiesole was first settled by Etruscans in the 7th century BC. The Romans who followed named the place *Faesulum*—praising it for its river bed and its ideal location for controlling the entire valley. Despite this, the town was repeatedly attacked by the Goths and Byzantines. In 1125 the city was destroyed by Florentine troops—only the cathedral and the bishop's palace were saved. Thus the city lost both its autonomy and its economic and political significance. During the 15th century Fiesole was a suburb where wealthy Florentines built their villas—and this fact has remained unchanged to this day. A villa in Fiesole, on the slopes of the hill, is one of *the* exclusive addresses. At the same time the town has managed to preserve a village-like character—especially above Piazza Mino.

Today **Fiesole** is the place to go for an outing—escaping from the oppressive heat on hot summer evenings

or from the hurly-burly of the city. You have the choice of either taking a taxi (note: the drivers charge extra because Fiesole lies outside the Florence city limits) or taking Bus No 7 from Piazza Stazuione, from the Cathedral or from Piazza San Marco, which takes about 35 minutes. Another alternative (for the very energetic) is to rent a bicycle. The views from the car or bus on the way up reveal a landscape of extraordinary beauty, dotted with numerous villas perched on the slope of the hill.

Arriving at **Piazza Mino da Fiesole** the first thing you will notice is the **Duomo di San Romolo**, begun in 1028 and thoroughly renovated in 1878. Some of the capitals are Roman. Across the way you can see the episcopal palace, which dates back to the 11th century, with a façade that was finished in 1675. Further up the square, the **Palazzo Pretorio**, with its coats of arms and emblems, goes back to the 14th century; the equestrian statue in front of it commemorates the encounter between Vittorio Emanuele II and Garibaldi.

Next to the Palazzo Pretorio you will find the small church of **Santa Maria Primerana**, originally mediaeval but rebuilt in the 16th

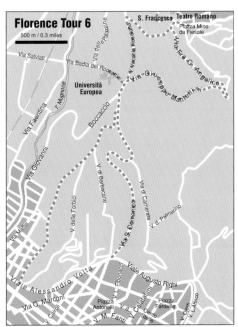

Roman ruins in Fiesole

century. Inside you will discover frescoes and a 14th-century crucifix. The church was designed for ordinary people, whereas the cathedral was used for ceremonies and special celebrations.

Following **Via Portigiani** will take you to the well-preserved **Roman amphitheatre** built in the 1st century BC and capable of holding up to 3,000 spectators (open 9am–7pm, in the winter from 10am–4pm; closed on holidays). The thermal baths to the right of the theatre are still equipped with a large tub, the remnants of the heating installations and components of the facilities, such as the *calidarium, sudarium, tepidarium* and the *frigidarium*. There are two altars in front of the Roman temple: the larger being Roman, the smaller Etruscan. The theatre is the venue of the *Estate Fiesolana,* a cultural festival held from June through August. Attending a performance is highly recommended, if only for the setting (a sweater is a must!).

San Francesco

The adjoining **Museo Civico** presents Roman and Etruscan material recovered from excavations. The **Museo Bandini** in Via Dupre' 1 features paintings and sculpture, majolica and furniture (open May–September: 10–12am, 3–

7pm; from October–April: 10–12.30am, 2.30–6pm). If you are not all that interested in history, I suggest you skip these two museums and spend the time enjoying the surrounding *campagna*.

An absolute must, on the other hand, is the walk up to **San Francesco**. The narrow, steep road (Via di San Francesco; to the right the restaurant **La Loggia degli Etruschi** has a pretty view) begins across from the façade of the cathedral and features two lookout points (the first toward the east, the second toward the south). The view of the valley with Florence and the Arno winding its way among the hills is unique. The boring neoclassical façade of the church of **Sant' Alessandro** hides a more exciting interior: a 9th-century basilica with ionic capitals and columns of Greek marble and a timber ceiling (open daily from 7–12am, 3–6.30pm).

Further up the hill, **San Francesco** was first a home for gentle-women before becoming a Franciscan monastery in 1399. At the beginning of this century the buildings were renovated a bit too thoroughly, but the overall impression of the church, cloister and monastery cells is quite convincing. The museum run by the Franciscan Order displays missionaries' souvenirs from all over the world.

Now it is time to head back down to the piazza for a well-deserved breather: the square has no shortage of bars and cafés. We will take another route on the way back to Florence: the hikers among us should go on foot; the less athletic can ask a taxi driver to follow this route which the bus does not take. Following **Via Vecchia Fiesolana**, we arrive at **S Domenico**. This church features frescoes by Beato Angelico, who lived here before he transferred to San Marco in Florence. A detour to the right, down **Via dei Roccettini**, will take you to **Badia Fiesolana**—the seat of the European University since 1973. Back at S Domenico you can either take Bus No 7 or—if you still have the stamina—walk back along **Via della Piazzola**, a narrow lane lined with old villas. From Piazza delle Cure, Bus No 1 will take you back into the centre of town.

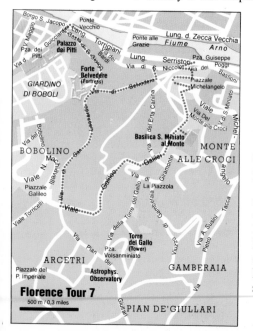

TOUR 7

The Other Side

Viali de Colli; to Piazzale Michelangelo; returning via Via San Leonardo with Forte Belvedere; to San Niccolo'.

For this walking tour you should wear your most comfortable shoes. From **Piazza G. Poggi** we climb the stairs (*rampe*) to **Piazzale Michelangelo** (Bus No 13 will also take you there), providing one of the finest views of the entire city. Beyond town you can see the hills around Fiesole and Settignano and on a clear day the peaks of the Apuan Alps are visible to the west. On Sundays the square is transformed into a meeting place for youngsters on motorcycles, families with baby carriages, daddies buying balloons, boys on skateboards, not to mention the ubiquitous tourists.

Further on up the hill we come to the church of **San Miniato al Monte**. The church owes its location to the fact that Saint Miniato, beheaded during the persecution of the Christians, was buried here in AD250. In 1013 a Benedictine abbey was erected here, soon followed by the current church which was completed in 1207. During the siege of Florence, Michelangelo protected its *campanile* (bell-tower) with mattresses against the stone cannon-balls of the Imperial Army. In 1553 the church was transformed into a fortress. During the 17th century it was temporarily used as a hospital for victims of the plague, then later as a hospice for the homeless. The geometric marble exterior is a typical example of Florentine Romanesque style, whereas the interior reveals an unusual arrangement influenced by Byzantine models.

Next we stroll along shady **Viale Michelangelo**, created in the 19th century by the urban planner and architect Giuseppe Poggi during the period when Florence was the capital of Italy. The **Café Fontana**, once a well-known artists' haunt, is a good place to stop for a rest.

View from Piazzale Michelangelo

Having caught our breath, we turn into narrow **Via S Leonardo** (beware of pickpockets on mopeds!) where many famous personalities have lived and where one still finds the most beautiful villas in Florence—surrounded by olive groves and yet only 10 minutes from the centre of the city. You can judge the hospitality and openness of the Florentines by the height of the walls isolating their villas from the outside world. On the right side at No 19, you will find the small church of **S Leonardo in Arcetri** (only open Sunday) with a marble pulpit going back to the 13th century.

Walking on, we come to the spectacular **Forte Belvedere** and its surrounding grounds. This fortress was constructed by the architect Buontalenti between 1590 and 1595, ostensibly for the defence of the city and of the Palazzo Pitti—then the residence of the Grand Duke—directly below. Actually, the fortress served to fend off danger not only *to* the city, but also *from* the city. One need not be a military strategist to imagine the advantages of this view of the city, lying at the foot of the fortress,

View from Forte Belvedere

in terms of suppressing possible uprisings. Each corner of the garden affords a totally different view: either of the city, of the hills or of the Boboli Gardens below.

Arriving back at the bottom, we turn left, passing through the **Porta S Giorgio**. This is the oldest city gate still standing (built in 1260) and it has a copy of a 13th-century carving of St George in combat with a dragon on its outer face (the original is now in the Palazzo Vecchio). Turn left and follow steep **Costa S Giorgio**. When Galileo Galilei lived here, he used to walk down Via S Leonardo in the opposite direction to reach his observatory in Arcetri. We arrive at **Piazza Santa Felicita** (the church of the same name features works by Pontormo) and **Via Guicciardini** to realize, suddenly, that we are already back in the centre of the city.

Another option upon arriving at the Porta S Giorgio is to turn into small, rural **Via di Belvedere** and walk down to Via San Miniato. On your right you will come across a pleasant old café with tables outside. Alternatively, you can have an ice-cream at the **Latteria Frilli** (Via San Miniato) or a glass of wine and a bite to eat at the **Mescita Osteria San Niccolo'** (Via San Niccolo' No 60), located in the San Niccolo' area, which has managed to preserve its old character.

You can wander back to the Ponte Vecchio along the embankments of the Arno, or look for the Via dei Bari, one step in from the river, a street lined with noble but austere 14th-century palaces, adorned with the coats of arms of their original owners.

Castle Hopping in Chianti

Through the Chianti region from castle to castle. Touring the soul of Tuscany (125 miles/200km) in two days.

Without visiting this wine-growing area nobody can claim to have been to Tuscany. In this ordered and harmonious, gentle yet austere landscape one finds all the elements characteristic of the Florentine Renaissance—the sense of balance and proportion, for example. You will also begin to realise how the Tuscan spirit was shaped by this hard yet fertile earth. Situated between Florence and Siena in the heart of Tuscany, the **Chianti region** derives its name from the famous wine: grown in an area covering some 175,000 acres (70,000ha), chianti is sold by 800 wine-growing estates. We are going to visit a few of them today, to experience the Tuscan landscape with its vineyards and olive groves, with its castles, abbeys and villas. With a length of 125 miles (200km), the entire tour can easily be covered in two days. To reach a few of the more remote scenic

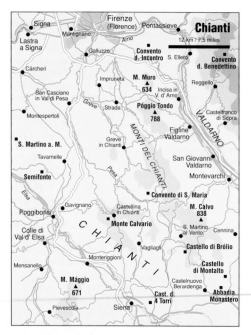

Chianti landscape

highlights, some of the shorter stretches will take us along unpaved roads. And as far as where to stay: how about spending the night in a real monastery or castle?

Today 'Chiantishire' is a truly cosmopolitan world: the English, Americans, Germans and Dutch began to settle down here long ago—joined by Italians who can no longer bear living in the cities of Milan or Florence. Who is not familiar with chianti, one of the most famous wines in the world? But who knows that the name is derived from the Etruscan family name *Clante* and that even the Etruscans knew the wine—although today's chianti is made according to a recipe created by the 'Iron Baron', Bettino Ricasoli (one third sangiovese grapes, one third canaiolo, one third malvasia).

Well, then, let us get under way: starting at **Piazza Ferrucci** in Florence we follow the signs to **Greve** or **Siena**. Beyond the town of Grassina, typical Chianti landscape spreads out before us. To the left of the road watch for the lawns of the **Ugolino Golfclub** with an 18-hole course (Via Chiantigiana Impruneta 3, Phone: 055-230 1009). Just the other side of **Strada** we take a left toward **Cintoia**. Already we can see the first mediaeval castle, the **Castello e Fattoria di Mugnana** (Phone: 055-858021). It goes back to the period of the Lombards and is one of the regions best-preserved castles. Here you also have the opportunity

A quiet spot

to taste and/or purchase your first Chianti wine. After a few more kilometres we arrive at the **Castello di Cintoia**, a Lombardic watchtower which is mentioned in records as early as AD996. If you look at the adjacent hill, you will see the late medieval **Sezzate Castle**. A couple of hundred metres on you will find a gushing spring, on the right, with very good drinking water. On the left side we see a riding stable, Il Poderino.

Having passed through the small town of **La Panca** (where there is a broom festival in June) we drive to the left and up the hill to **Badia Montescalari**. A word of warning: the road is unpaved and rather bumpy. We arrive at a fork: around the curve to the right there is a beautiful *casa colonica* with a church; heading on straight ahead we reach Montescalari, a former monastery belonging to the Vallombrosan Order and going back to the 10th or 11th century. Today, a millennium later, you can spend the night in a monastic cell and dine in the monastery refectory (phone: 055-959596). Up here there is a very pretty view of the surrounding hills.

The SP16 takes us to the main road, where we head left toward Ponte degli Stolli/Figline and, after about four kilometres, reach the lovely village of **Dudda** which, judging by the Roman graves that have been discovered, is most likely of Roman origin. Not far from Dudda we visit the **Castello di Querceto**, originally a

Lombardic castle, which was largely rebuilt after its destruction in 1530. Here you can sample not only red, but also white wine, *vinsanto* (sweet wine) and *aquavite* (spirits; phone: 055-856979). I recommend, however, that you do not try everything at the same time!

If the weather is clear it is worth driving up **Monte S Michele** (elevation: 2929ft/893m) where you can see a long way out over the whole region. Passing through **Lucolena**, a small sleepy village, we head on to **Badia** (or Badiaccia) **a Montemuro**, another typical village complete with an *osteria*. This marks the beginning of the unpaved stretch of our trip. Next we reach **Albola**, a village known as early as AD1010 but scarcely inhabited today. From here on it's downhill, through vineyards.

Next we follow the main road SS429 to **Radda**, one of the main centres of the Chianti region. This pretty town in the middle of wine-growing country is surrounded by a wall. We park outside and follow the main road to Piazza Francesco Ferrucci and from there to the Palazzo del Podesta' across from the church of San Nicola. You can taste and buy wine at the **Enoteca della Fattoria Vigna Vecchia** wine shop, 300 metres from Piazza Dante Alighieri. On the final Monday of each month a market is held in Radda. For lunch I recommend the **Hotel-Restaurant La Miranda** with its typical Tuscan atmosphere. After a strong *espresso* to fight off afternoon drowsiness, we head past the Villa Bistarenni Strozzi,

Badia Montescalari

back down the same road we came (approximately 10km/6 miles) to **Badia a Coltibuono**, an abbey and monastery belonging to the Vallombrosan Order (please ring the bell) and which goes back to the 8th century. If you did not dine in Miranda, the nearby restaurant now offers you an opportunity to do so (try the *grappa*). On the way back you can stop in at the *osteria* and stock up with wine, oil, *grappa*, vinegar, *vinsanto* and/or honey.

We now head for the tiny, marvellously renovated village of **Vertine**, then turn off the N408 to the **Meleto Fortress** (with an 18th-century theatre) which was frequently attacked because of its border location between Florence and Siena. Turning left 3km (2

miles) further down the road, our next fortress is **Brolio**, the home of the inventor of chianti, Baron Bettino Ricasoli. Regular tours are available (Sunday and holidays from 9–12am and 3–7pm, weekdays from 9–12am and 3–6pm; admission: 2,500 lire; pull the bell on the left). We drive back to the N408 and take a brief look at **S Giusto delle Monache**. We are now just outside Siena. If you want to avoid the city traffic, you can take a route by way of Pontignano—otherwise take the N408 along the periphery of Siena and then follow the SS222 toward Castellina in Chianti.

Five kilometres (3 miles) after the town of **Fonterutoli** you will come to **Castellina** (whose centre is blocked off to traffic), a city which, as its name says, was originally conceived as a *castello*, a fortified castle. It was meant to be part of a Florentine defence system stretching from the Elsa Valley to the Arno Valley. Further evidence of these plans is the castle of **Rocca**.

Following the medieval Via delle Volte, we head back in the direction of Greve in Chianti. First, however, make another stop in **Panzano** with its churches Il Vinaio del Chianti and Santa Novella. The most impressive visual feature is its irregular Piazza G Matteotti lined with arcades. Here you will find culinary delights and interesting crafts: ham and salami at the **Antica Macelleria Falorni**, ice cream at the **Gelateria Lepanto** or carvings at the **Bottega dell' Artigianato.** You can buy *vino sfuso* (open wine) at the **Azienda Agricila San Martino a Uzzano** (Piazzetta S Croce 47) or else wait until **Uzzano** another 2km (1¼ miles) down the road—where you can buy it directly from the producers. Our final stop this side of Florence is **Impruneta**. Its attraction is a very pretty pilgrimage church.

Practical Information

Hotels

This heavily visited region has an abundance of hotels and overnight accommodation. Here is a selection of the best addresses:

LOCANDO BORGO ANTICO
Lucolena—Greve in Chianti
Phone: 055-851024
Doubles: 50,000 lire
A group of buildings just beyond Lucolena, surrounded by hilly countryside.

HOTEL VILLA MIRANDA
La Villa—Gaiole in Chianti
Phone: 0577-738021
Doubles: 69,000–109,000 lire
Ms Miranda is a real local celebrity: after getting her guests full and tired with solid Tuscan food and good wine, she beds them down in characteristic, cosy rooms.

CASTELLO DI SPALTENNA
Gaiole in Chianti
Phone: 0577-799483
Doubles: 150,000–200,000 lire;
Apartments: 350,000 lire
An old renovated monastery with a Romanesque parish church. Really nice!

SAN FELICE
San Felice—Castelnuovo Berardenga
Phone: 0577-359260
Doubles: 190,000 lire
A well-known wine-growing estate: the rooms are located in a renovated mediaeval *case coloniche*—in a suggestive landscape.

RESIDENCE VILLA CATIGNANO
Catignano
Phone: 0577-282064
A beautiful villa with a view.

IL COLOMBAIO
Villa Ugurgeri della Berardenga
Quercegrossa
Phone: 0577-52450
Doubles: 87,000 lire
Family house of Count Ugurgeri della Berardenga; guests are served their meals in the Countess's dining room.

TENUTA DI RICAVO
Ricavo—Castellina in Chianti
Phone: 0577-740221
Doubles: 260,000–360,000 lire;
Apartments: 300,000–360,000 lire
This country estate is open from Easter to 20 October. It includes *case coloniche* and a swimming pool. For dining, evening dress is desired (no dogs or radios allowed).

VILLA LE BARONE
Via San Leonino 19
Panzano in Chianti
Phone: 055-852215
Doubles with half-board:
140,000–160,000 lire
This 16th-century villa is open
from 31 March–31 October. The
owner is a descendant of della
Robbia. Swimming pool.

**ALBERGO GIOVANNI DA
VERRAZZANO**
Piazza Matteotti 28
Greve in Chianti
Phone: 055-853189
Doubles: 91,000 lire
Very central location on the
beautiful piazza.

Restaurants

VILLA MIRANDA
La Villa—Gaiole in Chianti
Phone: 0577-738021
Tuscan dishes in a fitting ambi-
ence.

L'OSTERIA DEL 30
Villa a Sesta
Phone: 0557-359226
Closed Tuesday and Wednesday.
In the summer you can dine out-
doors. Large selection of wines.

ALBERGACCIO DI CASTELLINA
Via Fiorentina 35
Castellina in Chianti
Phone: 0557-741042
Closed Sunday.
A former barn. Charcoal-grilled
meat and homemade sausages.

OSTERIA GATTON BIGIO
Fonterutoli—Castellina in
Chianti
Phone: 0557-740212
Closed Monday.
Typical Tuscan *osteria*. The spe-
cialities are game, stuffed rabbit
and homemade sausages.

IL VESCOVINO
Via Ciampolo da Panzano 9
Panzano in Chianti
Phone: 055-852464
Closed Tuesday.
Terrace with panorama. Very
good cuisine. The building goes
back to the 14th century.

IL VINAIO DEL CHIANTI
(next to the church)
Panzano in Chianti
Phone: 055-852603
Closed Tuesday.
Pub, wine-tasting, live music;
vine-covered terrace with a view.

Shopping

You will find the best wine at
the following addresses:

FATTORIA DI MUGNANA
Cintoia
Volpaia
Radda in Chianti

CAPANNELLE
Gaiole in Chianti

ENOTECA MAESTRINI
Gaiole in Chianti

CACCHIANO
Gaiole in Chianti

FELSINE
Castelnuovo Berardenga

CASTELLO IN VILLA
Castelnuovo Berardenga

CASTELLARE
Castellina in Chianti

RENCINE
Castellina in Chianti

FONTODI
Panzano

SELVOLE
Greve in Chianti

CASTELLO DI UZZANO
Greve in Chianti

VILLA CAFAGGIO
Greve in Chianti

ENOTECA
Greve in Chianti

To go with the wine you should buy a real *pecorino* (*ricotta*, as well) from **Gigi the Shepherd** (to find him, turn left 2 km/1½ miles beyond Lucarelli, at Radda in Chianti). For excellent ham, try the **Macelleria Falorni**, Piazza Matteotti, Greve in Chianti. You will find hand-embroidered work for sale at **Nella Minucci** in Villa a Radda (just ask a passer-by).

Special Events

Castello di Montefioralle
MARCH: Sagra delle frittelle
(Rice doughnut festival)

Chiocchio
APRIL: Sagra del cinghiale
(Wild hog festival)

Panzano
APRIL: Festa della stagion bona
(Spring festival)

Greve in Chianti
EASTER MONDAY: Mostra mercato di picante e fiori
(Flower show and market)

S Polo
MAY: Festa del giaggiolo
(Lily festival)

La Panca
JUNE: Festa della ginestra
(Broom festival)

Panzano
JUNE: Sagra del re del bosco
(Forest King festival)

Greve in Chianti
SEPTEMBER: Mostra Mercato Vino Chianti Classico
(Chianti Classico wine-growers' festival)

Strada in Chianti
SEPTEMBER: Antica Fiere
(Old Fair)

Lucolena
OCTOBER: Festa delle castagne
(Chestnut festival)

TOUR ②

Maremma Amara

On foot, on horseback or by kayak through the nature reserve, Parco Nazionale dell'Uccellina; to the villages in the interior; a day of relaxation on the Argentario with its brilliant blue lake. 150 miles (250km). Three days.

This excursion is divided into three parts and will take about three days. Depending on the time of year you can give one segment preference over another.

'Bitter Maremma' it is called in one folksong. This marshland is famous for its horsebreeding, wild pig hunting and the austere villages of the interior. (Warning: in July there are *serafiche*, a tiny insect whose bite is terribly painful.) Today the land is very fertile in Maremma; even the Etruscans won extensive agricultural land by developing an ingenious irrigation system. The Maremma cattle, with their broad horns, are raised by *butteri*—real cowboys with strange leather trousers.

The Maremma region is very popular among Italians but one rarely sees foreigners here—yet. Maremman cuisine is highly praised and rightfully so, as you will experience for yourselves. Vetulonia and Roselle, those important Etruscan excavation sites, are also located in this region.

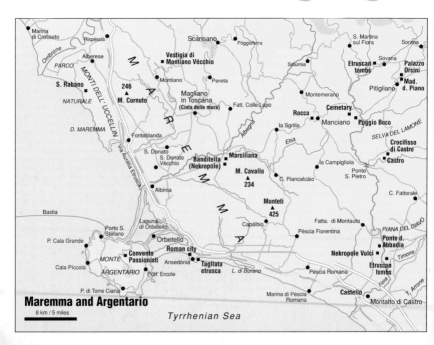

Maremma and Argentario

8 km / 5 miles

Tyrrhenian Sea

The swampy landscape of the Maremma

We will spend the first day in the **Parco Nationale dell'Uccellina** (Alberese, Ufficio Informazioni, open in the summer from Monday to Friday: 7.30am–6pm, Wednesday, Saturday and Sunday: 6am–6pm; during the winter: mornings only till around 2pm). Covering around 150 square miles (60km^2) this nature park is full of wildlife, including wild pigs, badgers, weasels and foxes. Birds of prey and water fowl are seen in large numbers and—be careful!—vipers, as well. The northern part of the park consists of beach, the southern portion is steep coastline. A variety of outings are possible: on foot, horseback or by kayak.

Passing Maremma cows on the bumpy road from Marina di Alberese, you reach the large 6-km/4-mile stretch of beach of Albarese—which is only crowded at the weekend in July or August. Parking is available and there are picnic sites with tables in the shade of pine trees. We can spend the night in **Talamone** (18km/11 miles from Alberese; the only accommodation being privately rented rooms), a small, still fairly picturesque harbour below the park—and our starting point for the next day. In Talamone itself you can climb to the top of the mountain and visit the harbour.

Taking the road through San Donato (Etruscan grave of Aurelia, to the left of the Grosseto/Rome superstrada) we drive to **Magliano di Toscana**. On the way you will come across various Etruscan gravesites and the ruins of Romanesque churches. Perched above an olive orchard, Magliano is a fortified mediaeval village, established in the 11th century. The Palazzo dei Priori (1430, Siennese style), the Romanesque church of S Martino and the Gothic-Romanesque church of S Giovanni Battista are worth seeing.

Beautiful Tuscany

The next stop after another 8 km (5 miles) is charming **Pereta** where you should stretch your legs. If you have developed an appetite, you can have lunch in the restaurant **Wilma**. After another 10 km (6 miles) of hilly countryside we reach **Scansano** with its narrow alleyways and steep stairs in the old part of town.

Next we drive to the popular and typically Tuscan town of **Montemerano** (21km/13 miles). Here there is a ring of walls going back to the 15th century and the church of San Giorgio, 1430, with frescoes and a pentatych. Soon after, coming to a left-hand bend, you will see the waterfall of the thermal baths of **Saturnia**. You will find swimming pools with thermal water in the hotel Terme di Saturnia. Stiff from all the driving, you can soak your aching limbs in the warm, soothing mineral solution. The ancients believed Saturnia to be the oldest settlement in Italy, which is why they gave it the divine name.

There is an Etruscan necropolis near Puntone, but the graves just before you get to Sovana are more worthwhile. Passing between flocks of sheep and herds of cattle, along steep slopes of red tufa, we continue to the **Temple Tomb of Ildebranda the Etruscan**. A three-minute walk from the road, it is something you should not miss. Passing through a tunnel the road takes us to the very beautiful, although heavily visited, town of **Sovana** (15½ miles/25km; SP22; up to the right). In this little tufa-stone jewel we should not pass up a visit to the proto-Romanesque church. Back on the main road, heading on past the Villa Orsini another kilometre, we come to a left turn to **Sorano**, which is situated above a deep ravine with a roaring stream and a waterfall. If there is no time left for this small medieval village, then take a right turn to a truly impressive place: **Pitigliano** (six kilometres) with the oldest Italian synagogue, the Palazzo Orsini (14th century) and the tufa caves where they cellar the local white wine—this you should drink in the company of genuine Pitiglians at Via Roma 53.

Continuing through the hilly landscape we reach **Manciano** and lovely **Capalbio** before crossing the Aurelia, and then on to **Lago di Burano**. If we are in luck and arrive by sundown, we will be able to witness a tremendous show. Depending on the time of year, flocks of migrating birds stop over here. The lagoon has been placed under the protection of the Worldwide Fund for Nature (guided tours). Before the sun has entirely set we drive on via

Ansedonia (Puccini Tower, Tagliata Etrusca) to **Monte Argentario**. This was once an island, but there are now three causeways connecting it to the mainland. This massif with a circumference of 25 miles (40 km) reaches an elevation of 2,000ft (635 metres). Mediterranean *macchia*, olive groves and vineyards prevail as green vegetation. Except in Porto Santo Stefano there has been hardly any speculative building

here. The coastline is extremely varied, but unfortunately rather inaccessible. 'Private' is the catchword, for this is one of the romping grounds, between Rome and Milan, favoured by the jet set largely due to the initiative of the town mayor, Susanna Agnelli, the Fiat tycoon's sister.

Of the two towns, **Porto Santo Stefano** and **Porto Ercole,** the latter is the prettier; it features a castle and a Spanish fortress. Behind Porto Ercole the coast turns back into rocky cliffs with small coves. For several kilometres the road becomes almost impassable except by jeep—but if you are not worried about the underside of your car you will be rewarded by a lovely landscape.

The road becomes paved again just before reaching **Cala Piccola**, a pleasant holiday village complete with hotel, and from there on to Porto Santo Stefano. Two of the few beaches which do not require great effort to reach are **La Cannelle** (approximately

Pitigliano

opposite Isola Rossa) and the beach to the left of the luxury hotel Il Pellicano, a couple of kilometres past Porto Ercole.

To really enjoy Argentario you would have to stay in a pretty hotel with a private beach, or else visit the peninsula off-season, when strolling through town is more popular than swimming. Not that the sea is not lovely. It is wonderful but, as I said, very inaccessible—except from a yacht. The small **Island of Giglio** is pretty with its inviting bathing beach of Campese. It can be reached daily by ferry from Porto Santo Stefano (in the summer by hydrofoil).

Practical Information

Hotels

HOTEL CORTE DEI BUTTERI
Aurelia—156km (Grosseto)
Phone: 0564-885548
Double: 300,000–460,000 lire
Open from May to mid-October.

HOTEL CAPO D'UOMO
Via Cala di Forno
Talamone
Phone: 0564-887077
Double: 70,000 lire
On a cliff above the sea.

L'ANTICO CASDALE DI SCANSANO
ss322—Scansano
Double: 122,000 lire
Riding stable and hotel. Rooms in former stables.

LOCANDA LAUDOMIA
Poderi di Montemerano
Phone: 0564-620062
View of the hills; very good cuisine, breakfast with fresh *ricotta* and homemade jam.

HOTEL TERME DI SATURNIA
Ristorante Villa Montepaldi
Club Benessere
Saturnia
Phone: 0564-601061
Double: 318,000 lire
Luxury hotel with all the frills. Everything for body and health.

HOTEL VILLA CLODIA
Via Italia 43
Saturnia
Phone: 0564-601212
Double: 79,500 lire
Central location. Lovely view
and swimming pool.

**ALBERGO RISTORANTE TAVERNA
ETRUSCA**
Piazza del Pretorio 16
Sovana
Phone: 0564-616183
Double: 62,000 lire
On the beautiful main square of
Sovona. Certain dishes are pre-
pared at the fireplace under the
eyes of the hungry guests.

TORRE CALAPICCOLA
Cala Piccola—Monte Argen-
tario
Phone: 0564-825144
Apartment: 105,000 lire per
person
Open April to mid-October.
Hotel in a tower, otherwise holiday apartments. Swimming
pools, restaurant, lovely location, choice view of the adjacent
island, Giglio.

DON PEDRO
Via Panoramica 23
Porto Ercole
Phone: 0564-833914
Double: 83,000 lire

IL PELLICANO
Sbarcatello—Porto Ercole
Phone: 0564-833801
Double: 250,000–410,000 lire
Open Easter–October.
Exclusive, beautiful location
with tennis and swimming.

Restaurants

TRATTORIA DA WILMA
Via Roma
Pereta
Phone: 0564-908079
Closed Thursday.
Top home-style cooking.

LOCANDA LAUDOMIA
Poderi di Montemerano
Phone: 0564-620062
Closed Tuesday.
Very good cuisine; excellent local
specialities.

CAINO
Via della Chiesa 4
Montemerano
Phone: 0564-602817
Closed Wednesday. Very good!

TAVERNA ETRUSCA
Piazza del Pretorio 16
Sovana
Phone: 0564-616183
Closed Monday.
Local specialities such as grilled
mushrooms and wild pork are
prepared before the astonished
guests—one of the most exclu-
sive restaurants in Maremma.

Il Cavallino
Via Baschieri 36
Porto Santo Stefano
Phone: 0564-817649
Closed Monday.
Speciality: fish.

Il Gambero Rosso
Lungomare Andrea Doria 70
Porto Ercole
Phone: 0564-832650
Closed Wednesday.
Terrace with a view.

Punto d'Incontro
(Restaurant/piano bar)
Cala Galera—Porto Ercole
Phone: 0564-832032
Open every day during the summer; weekends only during the winter. Very 'trendy'.

Discos

King Lido Discotheque
Bar-Ristorante

Cala-Galera—Porto Ercole
Phone: 0564-833912
Open every day from June–September; Friday and Saturday only during the winter.

Shopping

Il Frantoio Andreini
Via Amiatina 25
Poggioferro (Scansano)
Maremma delicacies.

Maremma Maglia
Via Italia
Montemerano
Handmade wool and cotton sweaters in pretty colours.

Mons Ameranus
Via Italia
Montemerano
Antiques.

ASTANTE
Piazza Vittorio Veneto
Saturnia
Knitwear, suitcases, straw goods.

Miele
Piazza Vittorio Veneto
Saturnia
Honey, sold by the producer.

Marco Vincenti
Via del Duomo 17
Sovana
Antiques.

Special Events

Grosseto
1–3 May and **15 August**
Torneo dei Butteri
Wild horseback games: the players try to steal roses pinned on each other's costumes.

Tour ③

Volterrana

Starting with Boccaccio's house; the mediaeval City of Towers, S Gimignano; to Volterra and into the Tuscan Ore Mountains; Massa Marittima and the abandoned abbey of S Galgano. 150 miles (250km). A relaxed two-day trip.

Certaldo, come voi forse avete potuto udire, e' un Castel di Val d'Elsa.
Certaldo, as you must have heard, is a castle in the Valley of Elsa.

Boccaccio, *Decameron*

To reach Certaldo (Certaldo Alto) from Florence you follow the *superstrada* in the direction of Siena, taking the S Donato and Tavarnelle Val di Pesa exit. Poggibonsi is an alternative exit. The first route, however, passes through more scenic landscape. There is plenty of parking available at the Palazzo Pretorio.

Born in Paris, Boccaccio also lived for some time in the red-brick city of **Certaldo**. He died here and was buried in the church of **SS Michele and Jacopo** (13th century; both the exterior and interior are brick masonry, with della Robbia terracotta figures).

Boccaccio's house, where he also died, is open to the public and I suggest you take this opportunity to tour the house (**Casa del Boccaccio**, Via Boccaccio). This small town palazzo has a distinctly patrician air. It is quite an experience, especially its small rooms and its steep and narrow staircases. In fact, the overall austerity and dignity suggests anything but the excesses we associate with Boccaccio's stories. We may presume that it was in the upper, more airy loggia that Boccaccio wrote his later works.

Certaldo still looks the same as the poet knew it back then: a small world where time has stood

Certaldo,
San Gimignano,
Volterra,
Massa Marittima

12 km / 7.5 miles

still. You can readily imagine yourself in a totally different century: seeing a smiling Monna Something with flopping breasts and a jug on her head stepping out of a house... If only such day-dreams were not always abruptly interrupted by the nervous honking of some car.

Walking up the narrow alleyway to its end, you will discover the **Palazzo Pretorio** looming over the town. In its original form it dates back to the 13th century; it was then reconstructed during the 15th century (open 9–12am, 4–7pm; admission: 5,000 lire.) In the **Loggia** to the far right the Court pronounced its verdicts. Other points of interest are the courtroom, the inner courtyard and the dungeon with the graffiti of former inmates. From the rooms there is a marvellous view of red roofs and vineyards. It is now high time for a large, fortifying breakfast on the terrace of the **Osteria del Vicario** (Via Rivellino) before heading the car out of town again.

Putting another 14 kilometres behind us, we reach **San Gimignano** (you will not need the car to get around, so leave it at the parking lot outside the town wall). With its tall towers and the double circle of walls, this is certainly the most impressive mediaeval city in Tuscany—the town where Florentine, Pisan and Sienese influences converged and mingled. Prior to 1580 the city boasted a grand total of 72 towers—today there are only 15. As well as defending the city, the towers served as status symbols. No private tower was ever allowed to exceed the height of the Pod-esta Tower. In Florence as well as in other Tuscan city-states, when-

San Gimignano

ever the *popolani* (the middle class) acquired sufficient power, they simply tore down the towers of the *magnati* (the city patriciate). San Gimignano, however, lost its autonomy at an early stage—before it could smash the power of the patriciate. This is the reason such a relatively large number of towers were left standing for us to admire today. You can climb to the top of **Torre Grossa**, the tallest tower in town. The cathedral contains an astonishing cycle of frescoes by Ghirlandaio. The **Piazza del Duomo** (you may want to check the 'Travel Information' to the right of the cathedral) with its uneven surface is the cheerful centre of the city. Directly next to it is the **Piazza della Cisterna** with its curious fountain. Today six towers line the square which, following the sloping contour of the hill, is neither plane nor perpendicular. From the **Rocca**, the fortress, there is a terrific view of the strange, surreal landscape, the so-called *Crete* (clay earth) region. Driving out of town—on your way to Volterra—stop to look back; the view of the town has not changed in centuries.

Thirteen kilometres (8 miles) down the road we reach the N68 and continue to **Volterra**. This last bastion of the Etruscans against the Romans is surrounded by an austere circular wall, a reminder that the city was constantly at war with San Gimignano. The centre of town is dominated by the **Palazzo dei Priori** (1208), the oldest town hall in Tuscany (Via dei Sarti: open 9.30am–1pm; picture gallery with works by Luca Signorelli and Domenico Ghirlandaio). Via Giusto Turrazzo leads to the cathedral (12th and 13th centuries; frescoes by Benozzo Gozzoli) and to the octagonal baptistry.

Piazza della Cisterna

Taking Via Roma off to the right you will reach **Casa Torre Buonparenti** with its Pisan appearance, dating back to the 13th century. The tiny windows are amusing—they were intended especially for children. Via Sari will lead you to the little S Michele Arcangelo church and to the **Casa-Torre Toscano** tower (13th century). The fortress (1472) is now a prison and before you insist on a tour, remember: getting in is much easier than getting out.

The climax of any visit to Volterra must undoubtedly be the important **Guarnacci Museum** containing treasures of the rich Etruscan cultural heritage, which the archaeologist Mario Guarnacci began collecting as early as 1732 (Via Don Minzoni; open 9am–1pm, 3–6.30pm; admission: 4,000 lire). The Etruscans exploited the same alabaster deposits still being quarried today—they used this soft yellowish material to carve their burial urns. Looking at the lids of the urns today we see their mysterious expressions—the expressions of people whom nothing has surprised for centuries.

The only surviving example of Etruscan architecture, the **Arco Etrusco**, is overwhelming. From the **Porta Menseri** you look down into the abyss: the **balze** are a series of cliffs caused by erosion which have already swallowed up houses and churches and have almost pulled a monastery into the depths.

We next proceed in the direction of Pomarance and Massa (40 miles/67km). Taking the turn-off to Massa, and passing Saline, we then enter the boron spring area and the so-called 'Ore Range'. Its geothermal facilities and strange pipelines can make you think you are in a science-fiction film. At the **Valle del Diavolo**, Devil's Valley, you can make a detour to **S Dalmazio** (5km/3 miles), a charming, small village, or drive a kilometre

Group photo with pigeons

further to the ruins of a 10th/11th-century church or an additional kilometre to the Romanesque-Gothic church of S **Dalmazio**.

Situated further up (45mins on foot) are **Rocca di Sillano** (11th century; excellent views!) and **Montacastelli** (Terme S Michele). Ignoring Larderello on the left (look for the geothermal facilities here as an easily recognizable landmark), we pass La Perla (thermal baths) and drive on through a landscape which is now green again with chestnut and oak trees—passing the fork (SP11) to the thermal baths on the left. The N44 to **Massa Marittima** also turns off to the left. Probably of Etruscan origin, Massa Marittima was the birthplace of St Bernard and is located at the centre of the mining area. The Massa Mining Codex (1225), was the world's first legislative regulation for the mining industry.

Located on the asymmetrical cathedral square, we discover the **Palazzo Pretorio** (13th century) and the centre of this city, the 12th century cathedral. Besides the Romanesque reredos either by Duccio Buoninsegna or his school, it is worth taking a look at the Augustinian church (14th century) and the clocktower (1228).

Leaving Massa we drive back to the N441—with **S Galgano** as our final destination. We still have another 20 miles (35km) to go, but they are well worth it, I guarantee, and we must see to it that we arrive by sunset (preferably on a weekday) or very early in the morning. What is it all about? There, on top of a green hill, is the big secret: a Cistercian abbey, with sky where the roof should be. Swallows fly in and out through the windows, the floor consists of grass and all around: nothing but silence. Once, as I arrived, I heard Gregorian chanting from afar. As I 'entered', the monks were singing under a canopy of blue sky.

Practical Information

Hotels

OSTERIA DEL VICARIO
Via Rivellino 3
Certaldo Alto
Phone: 0571-668228
Double: 140,000 lire
Terrace and restaurant.

HOTEL LA CISTERNA
Piazza della Cisterna
San Gimignano
Phone: 0557-940328
Double: 91,000–99,000 lire
The best hotel in San Gimignano.

HOTEL BEL SOGGIORNO
Via San Giovanni 91
San Gimignano
Phone: 0557-940375
Double: 89,000 lire

HOTEL PESCILE
Pescille—San Gimignano
Phone: 0577-940186
Double: 90,000 lire
Panorama and swimming pool.

CONVENTO DI SANT'AGOSTINO
Piazza Sant'Agostino
San Gimignano
Phone: 0577-940383
Double: 25,000 lire
You should write to Padre Superiore a month in advance if you want to stay in this monastery. Small rooms but with a fantastic view.

VILLA NENCINI
Borgo S Stefano—Volterra
Phone: 0588-86386
Double: 87,000 lire
A small villa with a view.

ALBERGO IL SOLE
Via della Liberta' 43
Massa Marittima
Phone: 0566-901971
Double: 85,000 lire

Restaurants

BELSOGGIORNO
Via San Giovanni 91
San Gimignano
Phone: 0577-940375
Closed Monday.
Good cuisine, pretty view.

LE VECCHIE MURA
Via Piandornella
San Gimignano
Phone: 0577-940270
Closed Tuesday.
The best in San Gimignano.

LA TAVERNETTA
Via Guarnacci 14
Volterra
Phone: 0588-87630
Closed Thursday.
Good game and mushrooms.

VECCHIO BORGO
Via Parenti 12
Massa Marittima
Phone: 0566-903950
Closed Sunday evenings and
Monday.
Venison or truffle *crostini*.

OSTERIA
Vicolo Porte
Massa Marittima
Phone: 0566-901991
Closed Tuesday. Rustic ambience.

DA SBRANA
Ghirlanda—Massa Marittima
Phone: 0566-902704
Closed Monday.
In the mountains.

BRACALI
Ghirlanda—Massa Marittima
Phone: 0566-902063
Closed Thursday.
Culinary speciality: boar.

Shopping

ARAZZI DA INDOSSARE
Via XX Septembre 2
San Gimignano
Handwoven goods.

LA CERAMICA IN SILIVA BEGHE'
Via San Mateo
San Gimignano

LINEA ORO
Piazza della Cisterna 16
San Gimignano

AZIENDA AGRICOLA TOLLENA
Via San Giovanni 71
San Gimignano
Panoramic view from patio.

Museums

Palazzo Pretorio
Certaldo Alto
Summer: 8am–noon; 4–5pm.
Winter: 8am–noon, 3–4pm.
Closed on Monday.

PINACOTECA CIVICA
San Gimignano
Summer: 9.30am–12.30pm; 3–
6pm. Winter: 9.30am–12.30pm,
2.30–5.30pm. Closed Monday.

Museo d'Arte Sacra
San Gimignano
Summer: 9.30am–12.30pm, 3–6pm. Winter: 9.30am–12.30pm, 2.30–5.30pm. Closed Monday.

Pinacoteca
Via dei Sarti
Voltera. Open 9am–1pm.

Museo Etrusco (Guarnicci)
Via Don Minzoni
Open 9.30am–1pm; 3–6.30pm.
Closed on Monday.

Palazzo dei Priori
Piazza dei Priori
Voltera. Open 9am–1pm.

Palazzo del Potesta'
Pinacoteca/Museo Archeologico
Piazza Garibaldi
Massa Marittima
Open 9am–1pm; 3–5pm.
Closed on Monday.

Museo della Miniera
Massa Marittima
Open: 10am–noon; 3–4pm.
Tours every half hour.

Special Events

Volterra
JULY: *Volterra Teatro*—Theatre festival on Piazza dei Priori and other squares.
JULY/AUGUST: Crossbow shooting, Piazza de Priori.
First Sunday in September: Flag throwing.

Massa Marittima
A Sunday around 20 May and again on the feast of St Bernard in the middle of August: *Balestro del Grifalco*—flag throwing etc.
JULY–20 SEPTEMBER: *Mercato dell'Artigianato*—Arts and crafts market.

Tour 4

Pisa, Lucca and Garfagnana

Pisa and the Leaning Tower (see it while it is still standing); Lucca; ascent into the remote and undeveloped Garfagnana region and the Apuan Alps; to Carrara.

Pisa's **Piazza del Duomo** is better known by the name of 'Campo dei Miracoli', the Miracle Field. The buildings seem to shoot out of the grass, as if by some miracle: the gleaming Cathedral, the Baptistry, the Camposanto and the Leaning Tower—all enclosed by the old city wall. I recommend you rest on the grass and take your time studying the façade—the quintessence of Pisan ecclesiastical architecture (providing, that is, that the grass is not so packed that you will have to worry about being stepped on). Moving inside you will find a pulpit by Giovanni Pisano. The realism in the rendering of the figures in the scenes from the life of Christ is astounding. From the outside, the Baptistry loses harmony due to the tremendous variety of detail. The interior, by contrast,

The Piazza del Duomo in Pisa

radiates a simple elegance. The pulpit by Nicola Pisano is charged with such emotion that even the horses portrayed seem to weep.

The earth in the **Camposanto** (open daily from 9am–6pm), the cemetery with the white walls, was brought from Mount Calvary by returning Crusaders. The frescoes of the *Triumph Over Death* are shattering in their revelation of the macabre world of the mediaeval imagination. What a contrast to the landscape by Taddeo Gaddi. On the opposite side of the square you have the **Museo delle Sinopie** (open daily from 9am–1pm, 3–5.30pm) with its collection of frescoes (*sinopie*) discovered during restoration work after World War II.

Is it still standing—really? Construction work on Pisa's Tower went on for nearly 200 years, because its deviant behaviour became only too apparent right from the start. It has been tipping by two millimetres a year ever since. A few years ago the Italian government approved a 30 billion lire project to curb once and for all the Tower's tilt. Consequently, it is no longer possible to climb all the way to the top and take in the wonderful view.

The **Museo dell'Opera del Duome** (open 9am–1pm, 3–5.30pm) and the **Museo Nazionale di San Matteo** (open 9am–7.30pm, Sunday and holidays from 9am–1.30pm; closed Monday) are treasure troves of Pisan art. Heading along Via Santa Maria and Piazza San Felice, Via de Mille and Via Corsica you will reach **Piazza dei Cavalieri**, once the centre of activity in the Republic of Pisa. It was in one of the towers of the **Palazzo dell'Orologio** —so we learn from Dante's

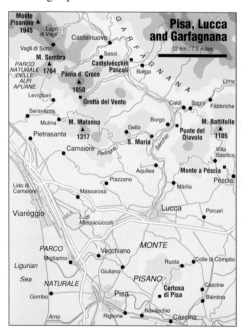

Garfagnana—untouched by tourism

Inferno—that a certain Count Ugolino, wrongly convicted of treason, was allowed to starve to death together with his sons. Turning into Via dei Consoli del Mare we come to **Piazza Santa Caterina** and its eponymous church. The **Borgo Stretto** quarter is the Old Town and is full of narrow alleyways. Arriving at the beautiful Piazza delle Vettovaglie with its arcade we can stop in at the **Trattoria La Mescita** for a bite to eat. Walking across the Ponte di Mezzo and then along Lungarno Gambacorti will take us to the church of **Santa Maria alla Spina**, a true gem of Pisan Gothic architecture (1230). Here, seafarers prayed before setting sail.

Opera fans on their way to Lucca can make the pilgrimage to **Torre del Lago Puccini**, to the Puccini villa on the Lake of Massaciuccoli to trace the *Tosca* composer's

In the Apuan Alps

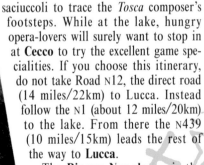

footsteps. While at the lake, hungry opera-lovers will surely want to stop in at **Cecco** to try the excellent game specialities. If you choose this itinerary, do not take Road N12, the direct road (14 miles/22km) to Lucca. Instead follow the N1 (about 12 miles/20km) to the lake. From there the N439 (10 miles/15km) leads the rest of the way to **Lucca**.

The **Piazza Napoleone** is the lively centre of Lucca; you'll find it quieter on the **Piazza San Martino**, reached by way of Via del Duomo, where the asymmetrical **cathedral** seems to be leaning on its *campanile* (belltower). Inside you will find works by Nicola Pisano, as well as the famous *Tomb of Ilaria del Carretto* by Jacopo della Quercia, one of the most significant achievements of Italian sculpture. There are also works by Tintoretto and Ghirlandaio.

Heading down Via del Duomo, you will reach the **Piazza San Michele** with its typical brick buildings, where the annual *Palio della Balestra*, a crossbow competition going back to feudal times, is held on 12 July. The church **San Michele in Foro** is rendered in Pisan-Lucchese style with holy pictures by Filippo Lippi inside.

Afterwards, tired as we are, let us visit the former pharmacy **Massa** (Piazza San Michele) for a fortifying glass of wine. Alternatively, we can stop off on Via Fillungo for a *biadina* with pine nuts floating in it. This is served at the **Antico Caffe' di Simo**—where any evening you can watch half of Lucca strolling by. A bit further on, at the Piazza Scarpellini, we can scrutinize the mummy of Saint Zita in the Romanesque church of **San Frediano**, where each 26 April she is taken out and celebrated. Next, our route takes us by way of the oval Piazza Anfiteatro and Via A Mondoni onto **Via Guinigi**, where the mediaeval palazzi with their red brickwork and white marble columns are still well preserved. The tower of the Palazzo Guinigi offers a good view (summer: Monday–Saturday 9am–5pm; winter: 10am–5pm).

Winding up our tour, we can walk along the imposing city wall, gaining a different impression of Lucca with each new perspective (you can also do this stretch by bicycle: Casermetta Santa Croce bicycle rentals, phone: 0583-587857; northwest of the wall).

If you happen to be travelling with children, you can take an interesting detour from Lucca, heading out on the N435 to **Collodi**, the birthplace of Pinocchio—where the various phases in the life of that little wooden rogue are portrayed as scenes in a large theme park. Otherwise, you follow the N12 (5 miles/8km) out of Lucca until you take the turn-off to **Marila**. Look for the royal **Villa Orsetti Pecci-Blunt** with its gorgeous park at the foot of a hill. Among the guests of this villa were Niccolo Paganini and Prince Metternich. The area around here is dotted with beautiful villas, known as the Ville Lucchesi.

This is the beginning of the **Garfagnana** region, stretching out on both sides of the River Serchio, between the Apuan Alps and the Apennines. This inaccessible and remote region was isolated from the rest of Tuscany for centuries and popular traditions long lost elsewhere have been preserved here. For example, the epic *maggi*, which originally welcomed the beginning of sum-

Ponte del Diavolo

mer, are still performed, as are various Christmas plays and the *sacre rappresentazioni* at Easter. Don't expect tremendous works of art. Instead the region offers wild, unadulterated nature, as well as a cultural tradition all its own, presenting a different, unexpected face of Tuscany—even to those who thought they already knew it.

Back on the N2 we head in the direction of Borgo a Mozzano; coming up on the right there is a turn-off to the Romanesque church of **Pieve di Brancoli**. If you miss it, you can take a look at Pieve S Donato in **Domazzano** or the isolated Pieve di S Maria (13th century) in **Diecimo,** both to the left of the road on the other bank of the Serchio. Back on the road, once you have passed Borgo a Mozzano on the left bank of the Serchio, you will come to a bridge whose daring design is truly amazing: the **Ponte del Diavolo**. This strange construction goes back to the 14th century. A legend has it that the builder appealed to the Devil himself for assistance; Satan supposedly demanded the soul of the first to cross the bridge as payment. The bridge builder—the Pontifex—who made this pact with the Devil, tricked the Evil One. The first to cross the bridge was a dog—helped on its way by a swift kick in the backside from the Pontifex.

But let's hurry on, back across the river. It's another seven kilometres on the N12, to **Bagni di Lucca**. In the 18th and 19th centuries, these old thermal baths were particularly popular among English poets because of the therapeutic effects of the warm, sulfurous waters. Shelley, Heine, Byron and the Brownings bathed here. The water seems to work wonders on paralysis.

From Bagni di Lucca there is a paved road to the picturesque, high-lying village of **Montefegatesi**, and from here you can reach the dreaded white-water gorge **Orrido di Botri**. There are two paths leading to the ravine: an easy trail from the parking lot (with nearby picnic grounds) and another from the **Rifugio Losentini**, which can only be recommended to very experienced mountaineering and climbing fanatics. Back on the N445 there is another temptation in store: picturesque **Coreglia Antelminelli**, surrounded by chestnut woods. Among other things, it includes an interesting arts and crafts museum featuring the plaster figures characteristic of this area. In addition, there are two churches, both Romanesque, **S Martino** (9th century) and **S Michele** (12th century).

The next stop on our tour is the beautiful and fash-

Calomini Cloister

ionable city of **Barga.** Parking our car outside the city wall, we enter through the city gate and head to the left through the narrow, winding streets with their palazzi modelled after those in Florence. The historic **Bar Capretz** is where the city's *noblesse* has met for a cultivated chat ever since the end of the 18th century.

At the top of the hill we reach—in the truest sense of the word—the peak of our visit to Barga: the cathedral **SS Pietro e Paolo Cathedral** (11th century). Its treasures are an extraordinary pulpit, the Lombardic polychrome figure of St Christopher, alabaster windows and the terracotta figures by della Robbia in the Cappella del Sacramento. From up here there is a 360-degree view of the Garfagnana mountains.

Now for something completely different: on the opposite side of the Serchio there is a road leading 9km (5½ miles along the Turrite brook to the well-known **Grotta del Vento** (Cave of the Wind) in the Apuan Alps, with 10,000ft (3,000m) of tunnels and caverns. The tour of the continuously changing grotto with its glorious colours takes a total of two hours. Assuming you are not claustrophobic, I think you will not regret the descent deep into this stony gullet. On our way back—before reaching the main N445—we turn left to make our way up to the **Calomini Cloister**, the home of a single monk, Frate Maurizio. Living here in solitude and silence, he shares this place only with the eagles and owls. What is the explanation for a Capucin monastery clinging to this rocky slope in the middle of nowhere? Supposedly, around the year 1,000, a small girl was climbing up this mountain when she found a picture of the Madonna in a grotto. Once they heard about this, the village inhabitants hurried to take the relic to their own parish church—however, the Mother of God did not fancy this and the icon returned to the grotto. The lively Madonna repeated this stunt several times until the peasants of Gallicano finally gave up and built a small church around the grotto itself.

Next we set out for **Castelnuovo di Garfagnana** where the poet Ludivico Ariosto spent three years as governor of Garfagnana. The **Rocca** is the most interesting site here. Next we have several options. It is unfortunate that we cannot do them all, unless that is, you have a whole week. The first route takes in: **Castelnuovo**, **Pieve Fosciana** (one of the oldest churches in Garfagnana), **San Pellegrino in Alpe** (shrine with a panoramic view and an interesting museum: 'Life in the Past'), **Sassorosso** (an atmospheric village of red stone from the nearby marble quarry), **Castiglione** (an impressive medieval village fortress), then turn left onto the N324 for **Carrara**.

The second route takes in **Pieve Fosciana**, **Castiglione**, **Villa Collemandina** (Romanesque church), **Corfino** (vacation and health resort at the foot of Pania di Corfino, elevation: 5,260ft/1,603m) and then on to the **Parco dell'Orecchiella** (inquiries at the Centro Visitatori). The park is full of deer, chamois, wild pigs, badgers, otters, weasels, eagles and buzzards, as well as 250 different types of flora. The return route is via to **Verrucole**, **S Romano** and especially impressive **Sambuca**.

The third option takes us from Castelnuovo along the N445 to **Poggio** near the beautiful and lonely church of **S Biagio** (1086). At Pon Poggio we take a left turn along a very beautiful stretch, to **Vagli di Sotto** and **Vagli di Sopra**, the oldest settlements in Garfagnana. In Vagli di Sotto the parish church of **S Regolo** is worth seeing. But the special attraction is the lake with the submerged village of **Fabbriche di Coreggine**—more or less visible depending on the water level. Sometimes the lake dries up completely, entirely exposing the village.

Then we make our way back to Castelnuovo and then right along **Turrite Secca** and along the Isola Santa lake (the church is in the water; sometimes you can see the tip of its steeple) towards **Arni**. Soon the so-called **Marmitte dei Giganti** ('Giants' Pots') appear: 23 huge holes (65ft/20m in diameter), a geological phenomenon. Some have steps for climbing in and out. Be careful: you do not want to wind up in the giants' soup.

The next leg of our journey is to the right to Arni, we then drive past the large marble quarries and on through the **Galleria del Cipollaio** carved out of the marble. From here the road leads down to **Seravezza** and **Forte dei Marmi**; an alternative route would take us from the Galleria to the right to **Massa** and **Carrara**.

Practical Information

Hotels

HOTEL CAVALIERI
Piazza Stazione 2
Pisa
Phone: 050-43290
Double: 309,000 lire

VILLA LA PRINCIPESSA
Massa Pisana (Lucca) ss12
Phone: 0583-370037
Open from 21 February–30
November.
Today the old patrician house
renovated by the Bourbon-
Parma is a *Relais de campagne*.

VILLA CASANOVA
Via di Casanova
Balbano (Lucca) SS12
Phone: 0583-548429
Double: 80,000 lire
March–October
Both rooms and apartments are
available.
Halfway between Lucca and the
sea: a working estate with vine-
yards and olive orchards selling
its own produce.

HOTEL HAMBROS
Banchieri—Lunata di Lucca
Phone: 0583-935355
Double: 106,000 lire
Old villa 9km (5½ miles) from
Lucca. The rooms to the rear
are the quietest. Note: breakfast
is not included and is as expen-
sive as an entire lunch.

ALBERGO VILLA LIBANO
Via del Sasso
Barga
Phone: 0583-723059
Double: 60,000 lire

HOTEL/RISTORANTE CARLINO
Via Garibaldi 5

Castelnuovo di Garfagnana
Phone: 0583-62045
Double: 75,000 lire

Restaurants

LA MESCITA
Via Cavalca 2
Pisa
Phone: 050-5442940
Closed on Sunday.
Tuscan ambience. Very good!

SERGIO
Lungarno Pacinotti 1
Pisa
Phone: 050-48245
Closed Sunday and Monday af-
ternoons.
Recommended.

DA GIULIO IN PELLERIA
Via delle Conci
Lucca
Phone: 0583-55948
Closed Sunday and Monday.
Reservations only; curious menu,
but very good.

ALL'OLIVO
Piazza S Quirico 1
Lucca

Phone: 0583-46264
Closed Wednesday.
Swordfish is the house speciality.

ANTICA LOCANDA DELL'ANGELO
Via Pescheria o Corte dell'Angelo
Lucca
Phone: 0583-47711
Closed Monday.
In business since 1414. Excellent
Lucchese cuisine.

VIPORE
Pieve di Santo Stefano—Lucca
Phone: 0583-395107
Closed all day Monday and Tuesday afternoons.

LA MORA
Ponte a Moriano—near Lucca
Phone: 0583-57109
Closed Monday.
Recommended.

RISTORANTE LUANA
Via Marconi 6
Barga
Phone: 0583-723315
Closed Tuesday.
In the summer you can eat on the terrace. Typical Garfagnana cuisine.

RISTORANTE CARLINO
Via Garibaldi 5
Castelnuovo di Garfangnana
Closed Monday.
Highly recommended.

Shopping

DA PROSPERO
Via Santa Lucia
Lucca

TADDEUCCI
Piazza San Michele
Lucca
Sells *Pan Buccellato,* a round anis cake from Lucca.

VINCENZO GUIDOTTI
Via di Piaggiori 119
Segromigno—near Lucca
Honey and fruit preserved in honey.

LIDO RICCI
Buetta di Pieve di Santo Stefano
Lucca
Locally produced olive oil.

IL CASTELLO
Via di Mezzo
Barga
Antiques.

MARCHETTI RENZO
Via di Mezzo
Barga
Local sausage and cheese.

IL GIGLIO GUELFO
Via del Pretorio
Barga
Ceramics.

CAMPOSANTO MONUMENTALE
Piazza Duomo
Pisa
Ceramics.

Museums and Sights

MUSEO DELLE SINOPIE
Piazza Duomo
Pisa
9am–1pm, 3–5.30pm.

MUSEO DELL'OPERA DEL DUOMO
Piazza Duomo
Pisa
9am–1pm, 3–5.30pm.

MUSEO NAZIONALE DI SAN MATTEO
Lungarno Mediceo, Piazza San
Matteo in Soarta
Pisa
9am–7.30pm; Sunday and holidays 9am–7.30pm.
Closed Monday.

MUSEO NATIONALE DI VILLA GUINIGI
Via della Quaranoia
Lucca
9am–2pm; holidays 9am–1pm;
closed Monday.

PINACOTECA DI PALAZZO MANSI
Via Galli Tassi
Lucca
9am–2pm; holidays 9am–1pm;
closed Monday.

GROTTA DEL VENTO
Fornovalasco—near Lucca
Phone: 0583-722020
Daily from 1 April–31 October,
otherwise only on holidays. Various tours—best arranged by
phone.

PARCO AGRITURISTICO LA PIELLA
Castelnuovo di Garfagnana
Phone: 0583-62916
With campsite. After hiking in
the chestnut forests on a hill
between Castelnuovo and Pieve
Fosciana, you can buy mushrooms, honey and chestnuts.

PARCO NATURALE ORECCHIELLA
Garfagnana
Phone: 0583-619098
Very interesting flora and fauna!

Special Events

Pisa
MAY and JUNE: Concerts.
JUNE 17: *Luminara*, the previous
day, when all the palazzi along
the Lungarno are illuminated.
The next day: the regatta.
26 JUNE: *Gioco del Ponte*, concerts.

Lucca
JULY and SEPTEMBER: *Palio della
Balestra*, crossbow shooting.
SEPTEMBER: *Settembre Lucchese
Luminaria di Santa Croce:* religious procession.
AUTUMN: *Salone del Cinema
d'Animazione*, animation festival.
Mercato Antiquario: every third
weekend. Antique furniture,
plates, cups, jewellery.

Barga
JULY: Music festival.

Anchiano (Borgo a Mozzano)
30 APRIL–1 MAY: *Sagra del Baccala'*, dried cod feast.

TOUR 5

Val d'Orcia

Monteriggioni and Siena; to the monastery of Monte Oliveto Maggiore and via Montalcino—where the famous Brunello is produced—up onto Monte Amiata; to Bagno Vignoni for a swim and via San Quirico to Pienza and Montepulciano.

From Florence you reach **Monteriggioni** via the *superstrada* to Siena; suddenly you will see the village, encircled by walls, as if straight out of a fresco by Simone Martini or Paolo Uccello. After a short walk we head on via the N2 to **Siena**.

Elsewhere in Tuscany there may be higher towers, richer museums—but the special thing about this city is that everything fits together. Siena shines in mediaeval perfection. In fact, as far back as the 13th century the builders endeavoured to conceive a whole into which the parts would fit harmoniously. Relations between Florence and Siena were never all that good: in 1230 the Florentines, witty as ever, catapulted excrements and donkey corpses over the Siena walls in the hope that their dear neighbours would die of the plague (a sort of forerunner of today's biological warfare).

Let's look first around the **Piazza del Campo**, a square in the shape of an amphitheatre. The cobblestones divide the Piazza into nine fields—meant to represent the *Governo dei Nove* ('Government of the Nine'). Between the nine fields 11 streets open out onto the square. In the centre of the upper part we have the **Fonte Gaia**

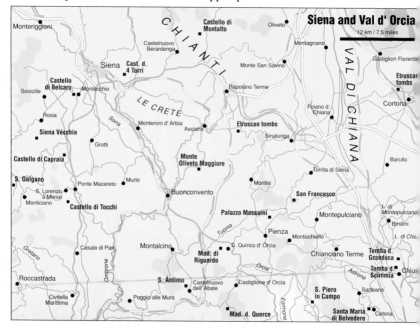

Siena and Val d' Orcia
12 km / 7.5 miles

View of Siena

fountain, a popular pigeon hangout. The **Palazzo Pubblico** is considered one of the most beautiful Gothic buildings in Tuscany (inside: Museo Civico, 9.30am–7.45pm; Sunday and holidays: 9.30am–1.45pm; Torre del Mangia, April–October, Monday to Saturday: 9am–6.30pm; Sunday: 9.30am–1pm; November to March, Monday–Saturday: 9.30am–1.30pm; Sunday: 9.30am–1pm).

Who will join me in climbing to the top of the **Torre del Mangia**? From that height there is a glorious view of the Piazza and the rooftops. You will find the statue of the Mangia, the gluttonous bellringer, in the **Cortile del Podesta'**. The **Cappella in Piazza** was erected in 1378 in thanksgiving for the end of the plague. The streets Via Banchi di Sotto, Via Banchi di Sopra and Via di Citta' divide Siena into three parts. Via di Citta' features the **Loggia della Mercanzia**, a temple of commerce, and the **Palazzo Chigi-Saracini** (seat of the Accademia Musicale Chigiana). Turning right onto Via del Capitano we see the Palazzo del Capitano di Giustizia.

The **Cathedral**—part Romanesque, part Gothic, because construction took so long—is perched on one of the three hills of Siena. Inside there is a pulpit by Nicola Pisano. To the left we come upon the **Libreria Piccolomini** (we will be coming across this name frequently during the course of this tour) housing the excellent il-

Siena Cathedral

Palio in Siena

luminated codexes of Pope Pius II. The frescoes by Pinturicchio
are not bad either. Other sights are: the Museo dell'Opera
Metropolitana and the Pinacoteca Nazionale ('National Picture
Gallery'); and the churches of San Domenico and San Francesco
(frescoes by the Lorenzetti brothers).

It is difficult, I know, to say goodbye to Siena. But there is
more that we want to see. Taking the N2 again—known as 'Via
Cassia' to the Romans—drive for 10 miles (16km) to **Buonconvento**.
Here we turn left onto the N451 and continue for another 9km
(5½ miles) to the monastery of **Monte Oliveto Maggiore** (summer
hours: 9.15am–12.30pm, 3–7pm; winter: 9.15am–12.30pm, 3–
5.30pm; otherwise ring the bell). As you approach, you will
already be able to see the brick-red cloister buildings glowing

from afar among the green cypresses
and olive trees. Founded by hermits in
1313, the abbey is still inhabited by
monks—so it is a place of reflection
and silence. The **Chiostro Grande** is
particularly interesting with its frescoes portraying the life of St Bene-
dict. The monks here still live as
they did in the 14th century and
produce their own wine, olive oil,
honey and herbal liqueur.

We backtrack the 9km (6 miles)
to the N2 (via Cassia) and drive
another 3km (2 miles) to where
the N323 branches off to **Montalcino**, a quiet town known for
the delicacy of its wine. As so
often in this country the land-

scape is simply beautiful. The fortress *(rocca)* is a reminder of the fact that Montalcino often fought on the side of Siena against Florence. On your way back down from the fortress you will pass an *enoteca* where you can try the exquisite Brunello along with the familiar *crostini*. At Piazza del Popolo look for the austere **Palazzo Communale**, at Piazza Garibaldi the **Sant'Agostino** church.

Five kilometres (3 miles) from Montalcino you can stop at the **Fattoria dei Barbi** to try the wine in the *cantina*—perhaps buying a bottle or two—and have something to eat in the *taverna*. Another 5km (3 miles) down the road we come upon the Romanesque abbey of **Sant'Antimo**, built in the 12th century on the ruins of a 9th-century church said to have been founded by Charlemagne.

It is a further 5km (3 miles) to **Monte Amiata**, a popular skiing area and another mile to a turn-off on the left to **Bagno Vignoni**. This little town is most evocative in the winter, when darkness is falling. We park. Then as we turn the corner, we are suddenly enveloped by steam. The yellowish light of the lanterns dimly illuminates the stone façades of the buildings lining the square. The vapours grow denser the harder we peer and suddenly the square turns out to be a huge basin full of bubbling sulfurous water. Before it was forbidden we used to swim here in the darkness of night, drinking sparkling wine. Now you have to go to the **Hotel Le Terme** (Phone: 0577-887365) which pumps the water from this historical pool—where even Lorenzo de'Medici and Saint Catharine bathed—into its own private swimming pools.

On the Piazza with the pool you also have the **Hotel Posta-Marcucci** (Phone: 0577-887112), said to be the work of Rossellino,

the municipal master builder of Pienza. Both Bagno Vignoni and S Galgano were well-kept secrets until Tarkovsky, the Russian filmmaker, used them as backdrops for scenes in his film *Nostalgia*. The remains of the medieval village of **Vignone** (10 houses, as well as a small Romanesque church, a well and lots of cats) are nearby (8km/5 miles).

After driving another 6km (4 miles) along the N2 (Via Cassia), we turn left to **S Quirico d'Orcia**, both historically and economically the 'capital' of the Val d'Orcia because of its location on the road built by the Lombards in the 7th century leading from France to Rome. In medieval times the traders and pilgrims using this route filled the hospices and monasteries in S Quirico, contributing to its development.

The masterpiece of S Quirico is a Romanesque church built on the ruins of a presbytery going back to the 8th century. The three terrible monsters on the architrave hardly contributed to dispelling the darkness of the Middle Ages. The 16th-century grounds of **Orti Leonini** are also worth seeing.

Ten kilometres (6 miles) further down the N146 we reach **Pienza**, the utopia developed by the humanist, poet and later Pope, Silvio Piccolomini. On the way to Pienza we come to **Pieve di Corsignano**, the 12th-century church where the little boy Enea Silvio, later to become Pope Pius II, was baptized. Here, too, note the demonic ornamentation. Here in the parish church of the former village of Corsignano is where Silvio conceived the idea of building a new town called the Pius-City of Pienza, according to Renaissance and humanist principles. The most significant buildings in Pienza—the **Cattedrale dell'Assunta** (1492), the **Palazzo Piccolomini** and the **Palazzo Pubblico**—are all on the main square, which is 50m (165ft) wide and 100m (330ft) long. In Pienza, by the way, you can buy excellent *pecorino* (cheese).

The road then winds upwards for 12km (7½ miles) to another small Renaissance town, one of the few hardly affected by tourism: **Montepulciano**. Having made the rounds of the Piazza Grande and the palazzi on Via del Corso, as well as San Biagio Church outside the wall, we can stop in at the **Cantucci** wine cellar near the Piazza Grande to enjoy the famous *vino nobile di Montepulciano* (0577-750006; open Monday–Saturday: 9.30am–1pm and 3–6pm). If you want to do something for your health, you can try the outdoor and indoor pools in **Chianciano** (9km/5½ miles), a health spa frequented by the ancient Etruscans and Romans (Phone: 0577-63167).

Hotels

CERTOSA DI MAGGIANO
Strada di Certosa 82
Siena
Phone: 0577-288180
Double: 265,000 lire
The oldest Carthusian monastery in Tuscany with frescoes and antiques. Swimming pool, tennis court and park.

TRE DONZELLE
Via delle Donzelle
Siena
Phone: 0577-280358
Double: 38,500 lire
Centrally located.

CASA DEL PELLEGRINO
Via Camporeggio 31
Siena
Phone: 0577-44177
Double: 50,000 lire
Rooms with views.

ABBAZIA DI MONTE OLIVETO MAGGIORE
53020 Siena
Phone: 0577-707017
Rooms in the monastery; written reservations required.

HOTEL POSTA MARCUCCI
Bagno Vignoni
Phone: 0577-887112
Double: 85,000 lire
Half-board; swimming pool with thermal water; rather ugly rooms.

LE TERME
Via delle Sorgenti 13
Bagno Vignoni
Phone: 0577-887150
Double: 60,000 lire
Atmosphere of days gone by.

ROCCOLO DI PALAZZUOLO
Palazzuolo—San Quirico d'Orcia
Phone: 0577-897080
Double: 70,000 lire
In lush countryside.

HOTEL CORSIGNANO
Via della Madonnina 11
Pienza
Phone: 0587-748501
Double: 79,000 lire
Modern barracks outside the old town.

RISTORANTE DA FALCO
(See below.)
Also rents out rooms.

Restaurants

You can eat well and not too expensively throughout the Val d'Orcia. The regional specialities are: *pici* a special noodle dish, hare and wild pork in sweet and sour sauce, *pecorino* and *soprassata* (sausage made of fresh course pork).

RISTORANTE IL POZZO
Piazza Roma
Monteriggioni—near Siena
Phone: 0577-304127
Closed Sunday evening and Monday.
Specialities such as stuffed pigeon, mushrooms, rabbit, homemade pasta and apple pie.

OSTERIA LE LOGGE
Via del Porrione 33
Siena
Phone: 0577-48013
Closed Sunday.
19th century interior. Typical Sienese cuisine.

RISTORANTE TORIDDO
Via Diacceto 1
Phone: 0577-282121
Siena
Closed Sunday evening and Monday.
Popular with the locals, inexpensive.

TRATTORIA TORRE
Via di Salicotti
Siena
Phone: 0577-287548
Closed Thursday.
Popular with the locals, inexpensive.

GELATERIA FONTE GAIA
Piazza del Campo
Siena
First-class ice-cream.

VECCHIO FORNO
Via Piazzola 8
S.Quirico D'Orcia
Phone: 0577-897380
For between-meal snacks.

ROCCOLO DI PALAZZUOLO
Palazzuolo—S Quirico d'Orcia
Phone: 0577-897080
Closed Tuesday.

DA FALCO
Via della Madonnina 2
Pienza
Phone: 0578-748551
Cosed Friday.

IL PRATO
Piazza Dante Alighieri 25
Pienza
Phone: 0578-748601
Closed Wendnesday.

CORSIGNANO
Via della Madonnina 11
Pienza
Phone: 0578-748501
Closed Tuesday.

BAR PIZZERIA CHECHI
Piazza Dante Alighieri 16
Pienza
Phone: 0578-748718
Closed Tuesday.

SPERONE NUDO
Via G Marconi 3/5

Pienza
Phone: 0578-748641
Closed Monday.

TAVERNA DELLA FATTORIA DEI BARBI
Phone: 0577-848277
Open 12.30pm–12.30am, closed Wednesday.
A wine-growing estate which also sells ham and salami.

LA CUCINA DI EDGARDO
Via Saloni 33
Montalcino
Phone: 0577-848232
Closed Wednesday.
In the middle of the Old Town, very chic.

Museums and Sights

MUSEO CIVICO
Piazza del Campo 1
Siena
9.30am–7.45pm;
Sunday and holidays: 9.30am–1.45pm.

MUSEO DELL'OPERA METROPOLITANA
Piazza Duomo 8
Siena
Summer: 9am–7.30pm; winter: 9am–1.30pm.

PINACOTECA NAZIONALE
Via San Peitro 29
Siena
.30am–7pm; Sunday 8.30am–1pm;
Closed Monday.

PALAZZO PICCOLOMINI
Piazza Pio II
Pienza
10am–12.30pm, 3–7pm; closed Monday.

PINACOTECA CROCIANI E MUSEO CIVICO
Via Ricci 15
Montepulciano
9.20am–1pm; closed Monday.

LE TERME
Via Dante 35
Bagno Vignoni
Phone: 0577-887365
End of June–end of October.

Special Events

Siena
JULY-AUGUST: *Settimane Musicali Senesi*
JULY: Jazz Festival
2 JULY and **16 AUGUST:** *Palio*

Montalcino
MIDDLE OF JULY: *Festival del Teatro*

Montepulciano
LAST SUNDAY IN AUGUST: Barrel race.

Elba

You should visit at least one of the islands of the Tuscan archipelago: Elba is the largest and has the most varied landscape. Once around the island and then a swim in a beautiful cove.

Nearly 30km (20 miles) long and 20km (12 miles) wide, and with 150km (94 miles) of coastline, Elba is the largest of the islands in the Tuscan archipelago. With its turquoise-coloured waters and numerous beaches and coves, it is no wonder that the island attracts millions of tourists every year. August is the worst possible time to visit this island; June and September are probably the best months, but spring begins here as early as March, when the *macchia* is in bloom. It takes a day to drive around the island.

Elba's first inhabitants were the Etruscans, who grew wealthy here quarrying the minerals. In the course of their history the Elbans have often had to fend off attacking pirates and buccaneers. The big event in the history of the island, however, was Napoleon's ten-month exile on Elba (see the **Villa dei Mulini** in Portoferraio and **Villa S Martino**, 6km (4 miles) from Portoferraio).

Geographically the island can be devided into three sections: the western, undeveloped part consists of a granite massif with Monte Capanne rising to an elevation of 1,021m (3,350ft)—with an impressive view of almost the entire island. The west offers good

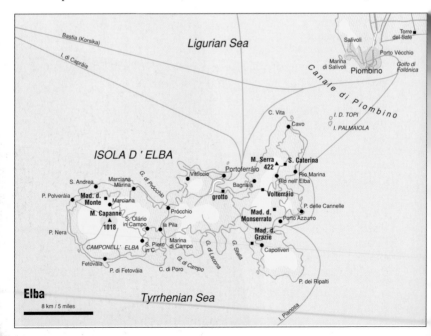

The impressive coast

hiking through lovely landscapes with alternating chestnut woods and *macchia* thickets. The coast is rocky and the coves are small but they make up for this by being much less crowded than in other areas. The middle section is more reminiscent of the Tuscany mainland: olive groves, vineyards and fruit plantations are characteristic features of the landscape.

The east is known for its deposits of iron ore and other minerals, which are still being mined today. The earth here displays a full range of shades. In addition to the cultivated plants widespread on the mainland, such as olive trees, cypresses and pines, there are also cork oaks, eucalyptus trees, agaves and palms. The *macchia* blossoms in more glorious colours than on the mainland. The sea is full of fish, much to the delight of divers and anglers. The underwater landscape is dominated by sponges and corals.

Like all islanders the Elbans have a character of their own quite distinct from that of the other Tuscans. In other words, they are rather nutty, but in a pleasant way. The Elban cuisine has its typical idiosyncrasies, as well. **Porto-ferraio**, our port of arrival, is an unusual place: despite the masses of tourists here year in, year out, it has nevertheless managed to preserve its original way of life. A third of the inhabitants of the island live here: in all around 10,000 people.

Assuming you have not already had your fill of churches, castles, fortresses and abbeys, you can help yourself to an extra ration here on Elba. For proof that there is plenty to see here, try the walk into the old town:

Fortress on Elba

from Piazza della Repubblica to Darsena, including the **Porta a Mare**, and then on to the Mediciesque **Torre della Linguinella**. For more lively impressions visit the **Galeazze Market** (Piazza Cavour), where everything that the island and its waters bring forth is offered for sale; or else check out the Piazza della Repubblica any Friday afternoon.

From Portoferraio we drive to **Rio nell'Elba**, a former fortress built for defence against attacking pirates. Situated high up on a rock, it is one of the oldest settlements on the island (a 6 mile/10km detour to **Cavo** will take you through a rather lonely landscape). **Rio Marina** (Palazzo Comunale, Collezione Ricci and Mineral Collection), the harbour of Rio nell'Elba, has a number of good restaurants. Next we head for **Porto Azzurro**, the island's second-largest harbour with two fortresses, Forte Longone and Forte Focardo; one of them being an infamous prison from which a well-known right-wing extremist attempted an escape, ensuring that all of Italy held its breath for several days. Further up you will find the totally Germanic, but otherwise pretty village of **Capoliveri**. Located south of Capoliveri, the **Fattoria Ripalte** rents out rooms, apartments and entire villas. The peninsula belonging to the Fattoria is at the private disposal of the hotel guests. This is one of the best addresses for an extended stay on Elba—provided that you are reasonably well-off.

Passing the touristic towns of **Lacona**, (large pretty beach: Spiaggia Grande) and **Marina di Campo** (unbearable in midsummer), we reach **Cavoli** and **Fetovaia** where there are good beaches. **Punta delle Tombe**, however, is less populated. From here we enter the 'Wild West'. If you can do without nightlife and the like, you will have a good time on this coastline, stretching from **Pomonte** to **S Andrea** (the view from Sedia di Napoleone is superb). For children the area is less suitable because of the lack of sandy beaches. From **Colle d'Orano** there is a path leading down to the somewhat stony but empty beach. **Cala della Cotaccia** is a comfortable cove with large, flat rocks. Behind **Capo S Andrea**, where the hotels are all rather ugly, there are several quiet guest-houses among shady trees. The **Pension Oleandro** also has a good restaurant with a terrace directly above the sea.

The road then makes its way up through chestnut woods to **Marciana Alta**, the oldest settlement on Elba. The beautiful church of **Madonna del Monte** can be reached on foot and a cable car goes to the top of **Monte Capanne** (otherwise take the footpath Sentiero N1—distance: 5km (3 miles), difference in elevation: 375m (1,230ft); two hours and 40 minutes from the steps under the Mediciesque gate next to S Lorenzo Church). **Poggio** is a small mountain village with narrow alleyways, known for its mineral water springs.

Back at the bottom we can visit **Marciana Marina**, a tiny harbour town (visit the Piazza Vittorio Emanuele) which is becoming more and more popular. Next we have the large bays of **Procchio** and **Biodola** (classy: Hotel Hermitage) with normally very clear water. From here there are two interesting detours: to **Capo d'Enfola** (including hiking trails) and to the small, pretty village of **Viticcio**.

Arriving back in Portoferraio it's time to make a decision: to cross back to the mainland or to jump on a ferry heading for the small volcanic island of **Capraia** 20km (12½ miles) away—complete with goats and a crater lake!

Practical Information

Hotels

ASSOCIAZIONE ALBERGATORI
Catala Italia 21
Portoferraio
Phone: 0565-914754
The place to phone/visit to make reservations.
Summer: 9am–12.30pm, 3.30–7pm. Winter: 8.30am–12.30pm; 3–6pm.

APE ELBANA
Via Cosimo dei Medici 1
Portoferraio
Phone: 0565-914245
Double: 60,000–68,000 lire.

PENSIONE OLEANDRO
Cottoncello—S Andrea
Phone: 0565-908088
Double: 43,000 lire

HOTEL DA GIACOMINO
Capo S. Andrea
Phone: 0565-908010
Double: 120,000 lire

LOCANDA DELL'AMICIZIA
Vallebuia, 1km from Seccheto
Phone: 0565-987051
Double: 50,000 lire
Lodgings and horses.

Fortress and sea

FATTORIA LE RIPE ALTE
Costa dei Gabbiani
Phone: 0565-935236
Apartments from 110,000 lire.
Open from April–mid-October.

Restaurants

LE GHIAIE
Piazza del Popolo
Portoferraio
Phone: 0565-914276
Closed Monday.

TRATTORIA DA LIDO
Salita di Falcone 2
Portoferraio
Phone: 0565-914650

RISTORANTE PENSIONE OLEANDRO
Cottoncello—S.Andrea
Phone: 0565-908088
Open April–mid-October.

PUBLIUS
Piazza XX Settembre
(loc. Poggio)
Phone: 0565-99208

RISTORANTE IL CHIASSO
Via Sauro, 20
Capoliveri
Phone: 0565-968709
Closed Tuesday.

Special Events

17 JANUARY: S Antonio: *Capo-liveri*—when horses and riders are blessed.

SUNDAY PRIOR TO SHROVE TUESDAY: Carnival in Porto Azzurro

1 MAY: Portoferraio: Parade in historic costumes in honour of Napoleon.

1ST WEEK IN JULY: Elba Jazz

TOUR (7)

Casentino and Arezzo

From the ruins of Romena Castle to Stia; the Hermitage of Camaldoli; by way of Poppi and Bibbiena to the monastery at La Verna; to Caprese, the birthplace of Michelangelo; on to Arezzo (Piero della Francesca) and Cortona.

The name **Casentino** refers to the upper Arno Valley, an area isolated from the rest of the world and as yet almost totally undiscovered by non-Italian tourism. From our starting point in Florence we drive to **Pontassieve** and then take the N70 over the **Consuma Pass** in the direction of Poppi, but 20km (12½ miles) past Consuma we turn off to the left to **Romena Castle.** Dante was once given lodgings here. The nearby 12th-century church of S **Pietro di Romena** is also interesting. Our next stop is **Stia** with its **Castello di Porciano.** We then take the N310 until we come to a road on the left leading off to the Hermitage of **Camaldoli** with its picturesque but gloomy location in a ravine. Founded in the 11th century, the monastery is still inhabited. The old cloister pharmacy with its mortars and crucibles is a pleasing relic of past times.

Unless you decide to stay and join the hermits you should press on via **Moggiona** and **Pratale** to **Poppi** with its majestic castle. A tour through the narrow streets, with their arcades and steep steps, is impressive because of the silent and dreamy atmosphere. Opposite the castle there is a stylish small hotel. Continuing on the N70 takes us to **Bibbiena**, mainly known for its salami. Then we turn left onto the N208 to reach **La Verna** (14th century), a busy place of pilgrimage—it was here that St. Francis of Assisi received the stigma in 1224. From here it is another 15km (9 miles) to **Caprese Michelangelo**, where it is possible to tour the very secluded house where the artist was born. We backtrack to **Chiusi di Verna**, then head on via **Chitignano** to the N71 and on to **Arezzo**.

Historical personalities such as Petrarch, Pietro

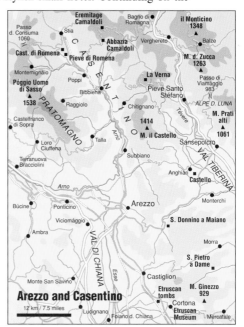

Arezzo and Casentino
12 km / 7.5 miles

Arezzo

Aretino and Vasari were born here—but they all left the city sooner or later. Only Piero della Francesca remained long enough to provide Arezzo with its one great attraction: the frescoes in the **S Francesco** church. The churches of S Domenico and S Maria della Pieve are worth a visit, as is the house in which Giorgio Vasari was born. On the **Piazza Grande** we can admire some magnificent Palazzi. On the first Sunday in September this is the site of the annual mediaeval tournament pageant *Giostra del Saracino*. On the first Sunday of each month the *Fiera Antiquaria* is held here, when antique dealers, private collectors and bargain-hunters haggle over the prices of more or less old artefacts and *objets d'art*.

The next stage of our journey is full of beautiful scenery: from Arezzo via Palazzo di Pero to **Castiglion Fiorentino** with its mediaeval circular wall. Just outside we come across the strange octagonal church of S **Maria della Consolazione**. Another four miles (10km) on and we reach the city of **Cortona** which already has quite an Umbrian air to it. Even upon arrival one cannot overlook its dominant fortress. On a clear day one has a fabulous view from **Piazza Garibaldi**, at the entrance to the old town, all the way to the Lake Trasimeno. On the Piazza della Repubblica, the centre of activity, the principal buildings are the Palazzo Comunale and the Palazzo Casali.

Let us make one final detour, taking us 1¼ miles (2km) outside of Cortona in the direction of Camucia, to the Renaissance church of **Madonna del Calcinaio.** On 14–15 August the *Sagra della Bistecca*, a huge steak blow-out, is held in Cortona. The city is full of barbecues and an unmistakable *bistecca* aroma; by the end of the night entire rivers of red wine have been guzzled.

If I may, to bring this to a good conclusion, I would like to venture a suggestion which I am not really authorised to make—since it does not lie within the bounds of Tuscany: the perfect finale would be a detour to **Lake Trasimeno**, taking the ferry to **Isola del Trasimeno** (lodging at Hotel Sauro). Have a great trip!

Practical Information

Hotels

GRAND HOTEL MINERVA
Via Fiorentina 4
Arezzo
Phone: 0575-357501
Double: 92,000 lire

HOTEL CONTINENTALE
Piazza Guido Monaco
Arezzo
Phone: 0575-20251
Double: 89,000 lire

ALBERGO OROSCOPO
Pieve Vecchia—S. Sepolcro
Phone: 0575-735051
Double: 60,000 lire

Restaurants

RISTORANTE LE TASTEVIN
Via de'Cenci 9
Arezzo
Phone: 0575-28304
Closed Monday.

RISTORANTE CONTINENTALE
Piazza Guido Monaco
Arezzo
Phone: 0575-20251
Closed Sunday.

LA BUCA DI SAN FRANCESCO
Via S.Francesco 1
Closed Tuesday.
Rustic restaurant; centrally located near S Francesco church.

LA FONTE DEI FRATI
Case Sparse 234
Camuscia di Cortona
Phone: 0575-601370
Closed Tuesday.

RISTORANTE AL PRINCIPE
Via Giovi 25
Giovi
Phone: 0575-362046
Closed Monday.
Speciality of the house: eel.

RISTORANTE OROSCOPO
Pieve Vecchia—S.Sepolcro
Phone: 0575-735051
Closed Tuesday.

Dining

Quant'e' bella giovinezza	Blissful youth with neither pain nor sorrow
che si fugge tuttavia	soon will be mouldering in the ground
Chi vuol esser lieto si	where no more merriment will be found
Di doman non c'e' certezza.	No one is certain about tomorrow.

Lorenzo il Magnifico

In Florence, you can eat well, for sure—but cheap is another story. Tuscan cuisine involves some of the best and healthiest cooking in Italy, although the selection of dishes is no longer as large as it used to be. It is an old and prudent school of cooking based on the preparation of spicy and tasty ingredients in an uncomplicated manner—thus their digestibility. This simplicity is more apparent than actual, for the success of this 'plain' style of cooking depends on proportion and balance and relies highly on the eye and nose. What is simpler than slapping a piece of meat on the grill, but who is actually able to prepare a true *bistecca alla fiorentina*? Even the Etruscans (as we discover on some of the frescoes) made fresh pasta and grilled chicken and other meats in the way they are prepared throughout Tuscany today. Even as early as the municipal era, Tuscan cuisine was more or less the way it is today—the essential features were established. And during the period of the Signoria, when Florence's trade relationships and banking activities had made it one of the most important centres of Europe, refined dining played an important role in Florentine commerce and culture. As early as the 14th century, at least a

hundred years before the rest of Europe, Tuscans were dining with forks. Thanks to the nationality and home ports of the discoverers of the Americas, certain spices, tomatoes and especially beans—all of these being basic ingredients for plain cooking—were quickly introduced to Tuscany. Through the chefs of the royal household of Caterina de'Medici, the wife of Henry II—and later through the influence of Maria de'Medici who married Henry IV in 1600—Tuscan cuisine even influenced the exquisite French cuisine: these gourmet queens, in fact, exported such delicacies as *canard a l'orange* and *soup d'oignon* to France.

Typical Tuscan dishes

The most noteworthy appetizers are *crostini* (small slices of white bread spread with a sort of warm liver paste) and *affettati misti*, ie *prosciutto* (the Tuscan ham is saltier than the better-known Parma ham), *salame* (pork sausage with coarse pieces of fat and whole peppercorns), *finocchiona* (a softer type of sausage with fennel) and *soprassata* (another type of soft, fresh sausage). As *primi* soups are more traditional than noodle dishes. These include *panzanella* or bread soups, a cold, refreshing summer dish, and *pappa al pomodoro*, and *ribollita*, the heavier winter dishes.

The noodle dish I particularly recommend is the delicious *pappardelle alla lepre* (fresh egg noodle strips with hare ragout). Simple but popular peasant dishes are *pasta e fagioli* (short noodles with beans, olive oil and sage) or *pasta e ceci* (noodles with chickpeas). For gourmets there are also *gnocchi* (small cornmeal dumplings) or *crespelle* (thin crêpes with various fillings), especially exquisite with *ricotta* (a mild sort of curd cheese) and spinach.

Moving on to the *secondi*: in Tuscany meat has priority over fish, and game is rightfully held in special esteem. In the Maremma they eat wild pork and hare; in other regions they favour quail and thrush. When it comes to pork the preferred fare is *arista* (from the Greek word *aristos*, the best): a piece of loin spiked with rosemary and garlic and slowly roasted. Or *salciccie*, pork sausages: some love them raw, spread on bread, others fried and with beans. Pork liver is wrapped in a net of fat, decorated with bay leaves, skewered and roasted. Chicken and rabbit are preferred deep fried, served with french-fried zucchini florets or artichokes on the side. We must not forget *trippa alla fiorentina*: tripe in tomato sauce. It is not dog food—I swear!

Fish enthusiasts will not want to miss the *cacciucco* in Livorno: get it while it is hot, because it is hot! Compared with this local concoction, *bouillabaise* is simply plain old fish soup. It is quite rough going for vegetarians in Tuscany: white beans, asparagus with egg, artichokes in *pinzimonio* (raw and dipped into olive oil leaf by leaf)—that just about sums it up. Of course, every restaurant serves the ubiquitous *insalata mista*, but that is about as Tuscan as Welsh rarebit. Our cheese *par excellence,* on the other hand, is *pecorino*—a sheep's milk cheese which today is almost exclusively made by Sardinian shepherds. In Tuscany shepherding is, alas, a dying profession.

Tuscan desserts are the *castagnaccio* (chestnut meal, pinenuts, nuts, raisins, rosemary, salt and olive oil), *schiacciata con l'uva* (puff pastry with black grapes), the plain *schiacciata alla fiorentina,* or *cenci* (literally: 'rags' or 'cloths', due to their tattered appearance). *Biscotti di Prato* (with almonds and dunked in *vinsanto*) can only be recommended to people with no dental problems! In Siena one should definitely try the mediaeval *panforte di Siena*: one cubic millimetre has more calories than an entire chocolate cake. *Zuppa inglese* ('English soup') is no more English than florentines are from Florence, or hamburgers are from Hamburg.

Well, do I dare to even begin on the subject of wines—with the vast variety available here? All right, then; white wines: *Vernaccia di San Gimignano, San Torpe', Montecarlo, Bianco di Pitigliano, Pomino, Bolgheri* and, well, maybe even the *Galestro.* As far as red wines are concerned, this task is more difficult. In addition to the various chianti classico wines which are practically all good, there are the non-classical types of chianti: *chianti dei colli aretini, dei colli fiorentini, colli senesi, solline pisane,* etc, depending on the specific geographical location from which the grapes originate.

Some red wines deserving special mention are: *Montescudaio, Carmignano* and *Pomino.* But the best (and heaviest) are the *Brunello di Montalcino* and the *Vino Nobile di Montepulciano.* The sweet wines include *Vinsanto* and *Morellino* from Elba. *Salute!*

Restaurants in Florence

International Cuisine:

AQUARELLO
Via Ghibellina 156r
Phone: 055-2340544
Closed Thursday.
Special, elegant atmosphere. Suitable for after theatre.

CAFFE' CONCERTO
Lungarno Cristoforo
Colombo 7
Phone: 055-677377
Closed Sunday.
On the Arno; *nouvelle cuisine.*

HARRY'S BAR
Lungarno Vespucci 22r
Phone: 055-296700
Closed Sunday.
Who does not know this place?

AL LUME DI CANDELA
Via delle Terme 23r
Phone: 055-294506
Closed Sunday.

RISTORNATE CORSINI
Lungarno Corsini 4
Phone: 055-217706
Closed Monday.
Tasteful elegance.

CIBREO (CAFFÉ)
Via dei Macci 118r
Phone: 055-2341100
Closed Sunday and Monday.
Haunt of celebrities; branch in
Tokyo; very good 'modernised'
Old Tuscan cooking in a pleasant
environment.

DONEY
Piazza Strozzi 18
Phone: 055-2398206
Closed Sunday; also Caffé
Exclusive; good service.

TAVERNA DEL BRONZINO
Via delle Ruote 25r
Phone: 055-495220
Closed Sunday.
Good cuisine, noble Tuscan sur-
roundings.

Basic Tuscan

BUCA LAPI
Via Trebbio 1r
Phone: 055-213768
Closed Sunday.
Typical cellar restaurant, walls
papered with newspaper.

CANTINETTA ANTINORI
Piazza Antinori 3
Phone: 055-292234
Closed Saturday and Sunday.
Typical Tuscan cuisine and house
wine.

Out of Town:

ALBERGACCIO SERRISTORI
Scopeti—S Casciano
Loc. S Andrea in Percussina
Phone: 055-828471
Closed Sunday.
Ideal destination for a trip out-
side the city. Plain cooking. De-
lightful wine. Rarely does any-
one exit the place sober.

SPAGHETTI

al pomodoro

Trattorie in Florence

ALLA VECCHIA BETTOLA
Viale L.Ariosto 32–34
Phone: 055-224158
Closed Sunday and Monday.

BORDINO
Via Stracciatella 9
Phone: 055-213048
Closed Sunday.
Conveniently located close by
the Ponte Vecchio.

ALESSI
Via di Mezzo 26r
Phone: 055-241821
Closed Sunday.
Excellent cuisine—also unusual
dishes and humane prices. The
catch: mile-long queues.

BORGO ANTICO
Piazza S Spirito 6r
Phone: 055-210437
Closed Sunday.
In the summer you can eat out-
side on the beautiful Piazza.

DA NOI
Via Fiesolana 46r
Phone: 055-242917
Closed Sunday and Monday.

The ambience is really nothing
special, but Da Noi offers some
of the finest cooking in town.

GANINO
Piazza dei Cimatori 4
Phone: 055-214125
Closed Sunday.
For a bite at noon, between mu-
seum visits and shopping.

IL CANTINONE
Via Santo Spirito 6r
Phone: 055-218898
Closed Monday.
Rustic ambience, no complete
meals, plain Tuscan cooking;
large selection of wines. Italians
rarely come in here—German
and American are the business
languages.

LATINI
Via Palchetti 6
Phone: 055-210916
Closed Monday.
It is really lively here. Totally
unsuitable for a romantic tête-
à-tète by candlelight.

MARIO
Via Rosina 2
Phone: 055-218550
Closed Sunday.
Opens at noon. Course, but truly
Tuscan.

Basic Tuscan

ANTICO FATTORE
Via Lambertesca 1
Phone: 055-261215
Closed Sunday and Monday.

COCO LEZZONE
Via del Parioncino 26
Phone: 055-287178
Closed Tuesday evening and Sunday.
A local tradition!

DI' CAMBI
Via S.Onofrio 1r
Phone: 055-217134
Closed Sunday.
In the characteristic quarter of
San Frediano; authentic Florentine cuisine.

LE CAVE DI MAIANO
Via delle Cave 16
Maiano—Fiesole
Phone: 055-59133
Closed Thursday and Sunday
evening.
Located outside the city,
and popular in summer.

SOSTANZA (DETTO IL TROIA)
Via del Porcellana 25r
Phone: 055-212691
Closed Saturday and
Sunday.
The best *bistecca alla
fiorentina*. Casual atmosphere.

International Cuisine

GARGA
Via del Moro 40r
Phone: 055-298898
Closed Sunday.
Currently very 'in'.

OMERO
Via Pian dei Giullari 11
Phone: 055-220053
Closed Tuesday.
Good cuisine, game specialities;
recommended as an escape on
hot summer evenings.

DANNY ROCK
Via Pandolfini 13
Phone: 055-2340307
Closed Monday.
Excellent crêpes.

ETRUSCA
Piazza Mino 2
Fiesole
Phone: 055-599484
Closed Friday.

S DOMENICO
Piazza S Domenico 11
Fiesole
Phone: 055-59182
Closed Wednesday.

Pizzerias

EDY HOUSE
Piazza Savonarola 9r
Phone: 055-588886
Closed Tuesday.

I TAROCCHI
Via dei Renai 14r
Phone: 055-2343912
Closed Monday.
Unsurpassed selection of *primi*.

Fish

CAPANNINA DI SANTE
Piazza Ravenna
Phone: 055-688345
Closed Sunday and Monday
lunchtimes.

PIERROT
Via Fra' Taddeo Gaddi 25r
Phone: 055-214005
Closed Sunday.

SILVIO
Via del Parione 74–76r
Phone: 055-214005
Closed Sunday.

Ethnic Restaurants

Florentines are not very daring
as far as their stomachs or
palates are concerned. Their
motto on this subject: "Cobbler,
stick to your last!".

Chinese

CHINA TOWN
Via Vecchietti 6r
Phone: 055-294470
Closed Tuesday.

IL MANDARINO
Via Condotta 17r
Phone: 055-296130
Closed Monday.

LAGO—SIU
Via Pisana 16r
Phone: 055-223145
Closed Monday.

Japanese

JAPANESE RESTAURANT ETTO
Via de' Neri 72r
Phone: 210940
Closed Monday.

Mexican

PIEDRA DEL SOL
Via de'Ginori 10r
Phone: 055-211427
Closed Wednesday.

Jewish

IL CUSCUSSU
Via Farini 2a
Phone: 055-241890
Sunday and Monday for supper.

Wine Bars

The wine bar: an old Florentine
institution which is almost dying
out. They also serve a bite to
eat: everything from *panino* to
complete meals.

ANGIOLINO
Via dell'Agnolo 107r
Closed Sunday.

ANTICA MESCITA S.NICCOLO'
Via S.Niccolo' 60-62r
Closed Sunday.

DA ZAZA'
Piazza del Mercato Centrale
Closed Sunday.

IL VECCHIO VINAIO
Via de'Neri 65r
Closed Sunday.

Shopping

In Florence, art has been closely linked to craftsmanship since Dante's time. From the former guilds of the *Arti e Mestieri* and the manufacturies of the former Grand Duchy right up to the present, the *botteghe* (once a 'school', now a 'shop') has always shown a high degree of creativity.

Naturally, not everything touted as *artigianato fiorentino* actually reflects this centuries-old culture and tradition. But, unlike almost any other city, Florence is the product of its mercantile capabilities and artisanship.

Tuscan Products

Characteristic Tuscan products are leather goods and objects crafted from straw and cloth. Ever since the Middle Ages tanning and leather processing have played an important rôle here. At the addresses listed below you can still acquire top craftsmanship—although not always for small sums of money.

You can buy leather and straw products at the **Mercato del Porcellino**. For exceptional silks pay a visit to **Antico Setificio Fiorentino** (Via Bartolini 4, San Frediano). At **Sylvia's** (Via dei Tavolini 10) you will find a tremendous selection of trimmings and bordering materials. **Giuseppe Lisio** (Via dei Fossi) sells most valuable materials.

At **Pineider's** on Via Tornabuoni 76r you will find stationary supplies—they hardly come any finer! **Giannini** (Piazza Pitti 37r) also has a lot to offer: leather handbags and cases or specially bound books and notepads. **Manelli Cellerini** on Via Santo Spirito makes hand-decorated cases and jewellery boxes. Handmade leather goods are also sold at **Il Bisonte** (Via del Parione 35r).

Even back in the guild era, the goldsmiths, silversmiths and jewellers played an important role: the Ponte Vecchio with its small shops is ample proof of this. Another interesting address is **Casa dell'Orafo** (next to Santo Stefano Church). If you want to meet the successors of the Old Masters of jewellery, stop in at **Mario Buccellati**'s (Via Tornabuoni 71r), **Settepassi Faraone** (Via Tornabuoni 25r) or **Brandimarte** (Via Bertolini 18)—to name but a few.

You would be hard put to find the following craftsmen and restorers on your own. For woodcarvings and such, you can turn to **Bartolozzi e Maioli** (Via Maggio 13). For something unique try **Ficalli e Belloni** (Via delle Caldaie 25), who produce *trompe-l'oeil* pieces in wood or stone. In the **Emporio S.Firenze** (Piazza S Firenze 8) you can buy cast-iron objects. For something a bit easier to carry, why don't you try **Emilio Paoli's** (Via della Vigna 26r), selling cane and straw objects. At **Paolo Pagliai's** (Borgo San Jacopo 41) you can have antique silver renovated or copied or order a set of table silver.

If you want something less 'cheap' to take home, I recommend the following Florentine antique dealers with excellent stock: **Guido Bartolozzi** (Via Maggio 18r), **Giovanni Pratesi** (Via Maggio 13) who specialises in the 17th century, **Alessandro Campolmi** (Sdrucciolo dei Pitti 22), **Giorgio Albertosi** (Piazza Frescobaldi 1r) who specialises in the 18th century, **Bellini** (Lungarno Soderini 5) and **Gianfranco Luzzetti** (Borgo San Jacopo 26). There are also many antique shops on Via de'Fossi and on Borgo Ognissanti.

Still looking for that extra-special souvenir of Florence? Try the old pharmacies, where you can indulge yourself in scents and essences: the **Farmacia Santa Maria Novella** (Via della Scala 16r) is worth a visit in itself for its frescoed interior and wonderful range of fragrant soaps, toilet waters and pot pourri. You can also try **Farmacia di San Marco** (Via Cavour), **Farmacia del Cinghiale** (in front of the Mercato del Porcellino) or the **Profumeria Inglese** (Via Tornabuoni 97r).

Books

The best places to go for books (in various languages) are **Feltrinelli** (Via Cavour 12) or **Seeber Messaggerie** (Via Tornabuoni 70r). The **Libreria Il Viaggio** (Via Ghibellina 117r) has the best selection of travel literature and travel guides. For art books and the like, try the **Libreria Salimbeni** (Via Palmieri 14–16r); for music books**: Il Fiorino della G.P.L.** (Via del Corso 43r). The womens' book store in Florence is **Libreria delle Donne** (on Via Fiesolana).

Hairdressers

While you are in the fashion metropolis of Florence why not try a new look at **Gabrio Staff** (Via de'Banchi 51r, Phone: 055-214688), **I Polverini** (Piazza Strozzi 4, Phone: 055-287354) or **Mario di Via della Vigna** (Via della Vigna Nuova 22r, Phone: 055-2398953).

Contact Lenses/Spectacles

If you want to be seen you need good (fore)sight: **Piancastelli** (Via Porta Rossa 48r, Phone: 055-210121) **Centro Ottico Fiorentino** (Via dei Pucci 4, Phone: 055-282794), **Ottica Fusi e Poggiali** (Via Roma 23r, Phone: 055-292235) are all opticians with top selections in quite central locations.

Couture

Nothing left to wear? This embarassing situation requires an immediate remedy. The first stop: **Gucci** (Via Tornabuoni 74r). Too conventional? How about shoes by **Ferragamo** (Via Tornabuoni 12r): they will not pinch your feet (almost as delightful as Birkenstock, but what a look!)—but maybe you are thinking of your wallet. **Luisa** (Via Roma 19r) has spiffy things. Or how about **Valentino** (Via della Vigna Nuova 47r) or **Emporio Armani** (Piazza Strozzi 14–16r)? Having an exclusive taste has always been a bit expensive. You could try **Principi** (Via Strozzi 21r) instead. They have everything from underpants to gloves. Or would you like to try **Emilio Pucci** (Via dei Pucci 6) on for size? Prefer something classical, after all? **Neuber** is on Via Strozzi 32. Even more classical? Then **Old England** (Via Vecchietti 28/2) is the place or **Ugolini** (Via Tornabuoni

20). Ladies, you can take your husbands to **Zanobetti's** (Via Calimala 20) and your sons (or boyfriends?) to **Gerard's** (Via Vaccherecia 18-20r). Something for the house? **Bruna Spadolini** (Lungarno Archibusieri 4r) stocks tableclothes and sheets of real linen. A silk nightgown to go with them? Then pop around to **Loretta Caponi's** (Borgo Ognissanti 12r).

Fine Foods

Procacci (Via Tornabuoni 64r) promises to please even the most demanding palates. Besides their famous *panini tartufati*, try the paté, all sorts of jams, tea, salamis etc, etc… **Pegna** (Via dello Studio 8) also has a wide selection in this category. You should also look around the **Mercato Centrale.**

Markets

If you like browsing around, then you might try your luck among the stamps, antiques and (more or less) fascinating junk at the flea market on Piazza Ciompi. **S Ambrogio** is a food market, also offering new clothes and flowers. The **Mercato delle Cascine** (Tuesday) is the cheapest clothing market; food is also sold. The **Mercato di San Lorenzo** (new and used clothing) is an institution—not even recent political pressure could get rid of it. The **Mercato Centrale** (Piazza del Mercato) is the largest food market.

Gifts for Hosts

Here, as all over the world, it is customary to bring along flowers, wine or chocolates when invited to someone else's home. Some good addresses to know in Florence are: **Mercatelli** (Via del Parione 33) for flowers, the **Enoteca Pinchiorri** (Via Ghibellina 87) with the largest selection of bottles and **Rivoire** (Piazza della Signoria) for the best in homemade chocolates.

Hats/Suitcases

After your shopping spree you are going to need a new suitcase:

Borsalino (Via Calzaiuoli 22r) and **Bojola** (Via Randinelli, corner of Via de Banchi) have a large array of fine leather suitcases and hats. For something on the smarter side, have a look at the selection at **Mandarina Duck** (Via Por Santa Maria).

Records/CDs

If you are interested in musical instruments, pianos, hi-fi, TVs, video equipment, musical books etc, you will marvel at the extraordinary range of products at **Ricordi** (Via Brunelleschi 8r). For more modern merchandise such as CDs, try **Alberti** (Via dei Pucci 10–20r) with its terrific selection of records. **Contempo Records** (Via dei Neri 15r) is a direct importer of records and cassettes.

Cleaners

You're in a sticky predicament:
with breakfast marmalade on your new shirt and
no fresh change of clothes. That's quite a jam! The **Lavanderia Lavaget** (Piazza Ghiberti) or the **Tintoria Fiorentina** (Via Palmieri 5r) may help you out get your act cleaned up.

Paraphernalia & Second Hand

At **Babilonia** (Piazza Mercato Centrale 37r) you'll need an entire afternoon to dig through everything! **Chez Charlie** (Via delle Terme) does not have quite the range, but is more selective. For very exclusive old things, try **Wonder Woman** (Via Alfani).

Sporting Goods

For sports kits and equipment, you can walk (or run) to either **Lo Sport** (Piazza Duomo 6–8r) or **Galleria dello Sport** (Via Venezia 18–20r). **Il Rifugio Sport** (Piazza Ottaviani 3r)—is only a short distance from the centre of town.

What to Know? Practical Information

June—or at least before 15 July when all the hustle and bustle starts. September and October are good months again, only expect a few rainy days.

TRAVEL ESSENTIALS

When to Visit
Tuscany is worth a visit in any season. However, since the region goes through many changes throughout the year, your choice of season depends on which Tuscany you would like to see. If your main interest is in art and architecture, you should avoid August when many museums and institutions are closed.

If your plans focus on close contact with nature, you should avoid the months November to February because of frequent rain, as well as August because of the flood of tourists—unless you stick to smaller towns and the more remote regions (Garfagnana and Casentino, for example).

The Tuscan hot springs are ideal in late autumn, winter and the beginning of spring. The sea itself is enjoyable from April to late September, but thrashing around in milling crowds in August is not my idea of swimming.

Touring the main attractions of Florence, Siena and Pisa around Easter is nothing but torture. If you prefer a bit of everything—ie art, sea and countryside—I recommend May and

Visa Requirements
Citizens of European Community countries require no visa. Other nationals only do so if they intend to stay longer than three months.

Airports
PERETOLA DIE FIRENZE (internal)
Via del Termine 1. Phone: 055-315642
GALLILEO GALLILEI (international)
Pisa. Phone: 050-40132.

MONEY MATTERS

First: beware of the many zeroes (on the bills)!
Second: in the larger cities there are pickpockets.
Third: in Italy *everything* has become more expensive than in other countries (except Japan). At the time of publication, the exchange rate is about 1,100 lire to a US Dollar and 2,100 lire to the Pound Sterling. Petrol costs around 1,600 lire per litre; the bill for an average meal is about 35,000 to 40,000 lire per person. A double room can hardly be had for less than 100,000 lire per night.

Fourth: in the morning banks have normal business hours (Monday–Friday 8.30am–1pm), in the afternoon they vary from bank to bank—most are open from 3–3.45pm. In large cities there are automatic exchange tellers; only in emergencies, however, are these worth the trouble, due to the adverse rates of exchange.

GETTING ACQUAINTED

Geography and Economy
Tuscany, with an area of 60,000 square miles (22,992km²) is the fifth largest region in Italy and has the shape of a triangle. Its northern border are the Apennines, the western boundary the Tyrrhenian Sea; in the south the complicated border is formed by mountain ridges, basins and plains.

Tuscany has nine provinces, 287 municipalities, a population of 3,568,799 with a density of 60 per square mile (155 per km²). The coastal strip from Carrara to Livorno and the lower Arno Valley from Florence to Pisa are heavily populated. With the exception of the interior comprising the Maremma, the Campagna around Siena and the upper Appenines, the standard of living is a little higher than the national average.

Agriculture plays an important role, especially wine and olive-growing in the Chianti region and the cultivation of grain and vegetables in the Maremma. Cattle are raised mainly in the Maremma. Industrially, mining plays an important role. There is also significant metallurgy in Piombino, Livorno, Florence and San Giovanni Valdarno. Leather is tanned in S Croce on the Arno, glass is blown in Empoli and small trades flourish everywhere.

Climate
One expects a Mediterranean climate —but these days nobody really knows what kind of weather to expect. In the last few years, spring has arrived much too early; then it wouldn't really turn into summer; then, in August, the temperatures would soar to 40°c/114°F making it unbearable, even in the water. After that not a drop of rain fell until November, and winter never got as cold as it should.

So: pack everything from swimming trunks to a raincoat—except a fur coat, which one does not really need here (for climatic reasons, at least— they are a must at theatres and opera where the distinguished ladies would feel a chill without one—even in May at the *Maggio Musicale Fiorentino*).

Time
Italy observes Central European Time (CET) with summer time in effect from the end of April through to the end of October.

GETTING AROUND

Car, Train or Bus?

The car is the most comfortable means of transportation for individual travel, but also the most expensive—especially with petrol prices at such a high level in Italy (see: 'Money Matters').

Bus and train require more time. The trains are usually so overcrowded one seldom finds a seat—unless one takes special trains like the Intercity, Pendolino etc. They, on the other hand, are considerably more expensive and do not stop at every town. The bus is an alternative to the car. Here are the addresses of the main bus companies:

LAZZI: Piazza Stazione 4-6r, Florence, phone: 055-215154

SITA: Via S Caterina da Siena 15r, phone: 055-211487

COPIT: Piazza S Maria Novella, Florence, phone: 055-215154

CAT: Via Fiume 2r, Florence, phone: 055-283400

CAP: Piazza Stazione-Via Nazionale 13r, Florence, phone: 055-214637

In Florence you do not need a car at all. It is best to leave it in the hotel car park or park it at the Fortezza da Basso. The car-free zone is nearly as large as the historical part of the city itself—ie the entire area within the Viali di Circonvallazione ring is closed to private automobile traffic. In the inner city there is a chronic parking problem—it is almost impossible to find a legal space. Besides, the centre of town is so small that it is much better to tour it on foot. You should only need the car for a drive to Fiesole. The situation in other cities such as Pisa, Lucca or Siena is the same as in Florence. By parking the car outside the centre of town you will avoid one major headache: the search for parking places through confusing one-way streets that can spoil your entire visit. In selecting the routes for our tours we have avoided all highways and *superstrade*, intentionally picking side roads which will allow you actually to see what you have come here for.

Maps

City maps are available at all kiosks and book stores; road maps and travel guides at specialist book stores, such as the **Libreria Il Viaggio**, Via Ghibellina, Florence.

Sightseeing Tours

For information and reservations, contact any of the local tourist agencies or alternatively try:

AGRITURIST, Piazza S Firenze 3, phone: 055-287838.

Public Transportation

There is no metro in Florence, because the Etruscans and Romans would roll over in their graves, and the tramway has already 'bitten the dust'. The orange **ATAF** buses are still alive (Piazza Duomo 57r, phone: 055-580528). Buy the tickets either at a kiosk or in a *bar tabacchi*; a single costs 800 lire for 70 minutes or 1,000 lire for two hours; with a 3,000-lire ticket you can take four separate journeys, with a 6,000 lire you can ride eight times.

Bicycle-Hire
COOPERATIVA CIAO E BASTA
Costa dei Magnoli 24, phone: 055-263985

Auto Breakdown Service
ASSISTENZA AUTOMOBILISTICA ACI
Phone: 055-24861 or phone: 116

Car Rental

AVIS
Borgo Ognissanti 128r
Phone: 055-2398826

EUROPCAR
Borgo Ognissanti 53-55r
Phone: 055-293444

HERTZ
Via Maso Finiguerra 33
Phone: 055-2398205

ITALY BY CAR
Borgo Ognissanti 134r
Phone: 055-293021

MAGGIONE
Via Maso Finiguerra 11r
Phone: 055-210238

AEROPORTO PERETOLA
Phone: 055-210238

WHERE TO STAY

Hotels
Our selection distinguishes four hotel categories and lists the price of a double room with breakfast. This price will also serve as to estimate the price of a single room.

Luxury Class

EXCELSIOR
Piazza Ognissanti 3
Phone: 055-264201
Double: 583,000 lire
Exclusive hotel with roof garden and piano bar; beautiful central location on the River Arno.

GRAND HOTEL
Piazza Ognissanti
Phone: 055-278781
Double: 610,000 lire
Freshly renovated, lovely salon.

REGENCY
Piazza d'Azeglio 3
Phone: 055-245247
Double: 530,000 lire
Belonging to Relais & Cheteaux, located on the quiet Piazza d'Azeglio, 5 minutes from the centre of town.

GRAND HOTEL VILLA CORA
Viale Machiavelli 18
Phone: 055-2298451
Double: 600,000 lire
19th century villa with a beautiful 'rural' location at the end of Viale dei Colli.

HELVETIA & BRISTOL
Via dei Pescioni 2
Phone: 055-287814
Double: 547,000 lire
Freshly renovated, in a central location.

SPUMANTE DI VERNACCIA

SAVOY
Piazza della Repubblica 7
Phone: 055-283313
Double: 550,000 lire
The most central, but noisy!

VILLA SAN MICHELE
Via Doccia 4
Fiesole
Phone: 055-59451
Double: 675,000 lire
Former Franciscan monastery built according to plans by Michelangelo. Famous for its panorama of the city.

Expensive

BERCHELLI
Lugarno Acciaiuoli 14
Phone: 055-264061
Double: 240,000 lire
Freshly renovated; beautiful view of the River Arno.

BERNINI PALACE
Piazza S Firenze 29
Phone: 055-278621
Double: 250,000 lire

BRUNELLESCHI
Piazza S Elisabetta 3
Phone: 055-562068
Double: 270,000 lire
A tower going back to the 6th century.

DE LA VILLE
Piazza Antinori 1

Phone: 055-261805
Double: 250,000 lire

GRAND HOTEL MINERVA
Piazza S Maria Novella 16
Phone: 055-284555
Double: 244,000 lire

KRAFT
Via Solferino 2
Phone: 055-284273
Double: 274,000 lire

MONTEBELLO SPLENDID
Via Montebello 60
Phone: 055-298051
Double: 280,000 lire

PLAZA HOTEL LUCCHESI
Lungarno della Zecca Vecchia 38
Phone: 055-264141
Double: 265,000 lire

TORRE DI BELLOSGUARDO
Via Roti Michelozzi 2
Phone: 055-2298145
Double: 270,000 lire
This quiet old castle with its few rooms affords a view of the entire city from a very special perspective. Highly recommended.

Moderate

ANNALENA
Via Romana 34
Phone: 055-222402
Double: 106,000 lire
Recommended.

BEACCI TORNABUONI
Via Tornabuoni 3
Phone: 055-212645
Double: 106,000 lire
Good location.

LOGGIATO DEI SERVITI
Piazza SS Annunziata 3
Phone: 055-219165
Double: 112,500 lire
Every room has antique furniture.

QUISISANA–PONTE VECCHIO
Lungarno Archibusieri 4
Phone: 055-216692
Double: 106,000 lire
Location for James Ivory's film *Room with a View*.

PORTA ROSSA
Via Porta Rossa 19
Phone:055-287551
Double: 106,000
Very centrally located; antique atmosphere.

VILLA LE RONDINI
Via Bolognese Vecchia 224
Phone:055-400081
Double: 106,000 lire
Large park with cypress trees and olive groves on the hills surrounding Florence. Tennis and swimming.

VILLA BELVEDERE
Via Benedetto Castelli
Phone: 055-222501
Double: 210,000 lire
Once belonged to the Medici.

CALZAIUOLI
Via de'Calzaiuoli 6
Phone: 055-212456
Double: 112,500 lire
Centrally located. Small but noble.

BENCISTA'
Via Benedetto da Maiano 4
Phone: 055-59163

LOCALITA' SAN DOMENICO (Fiesole)
Double: 65,000 lire
In a peaceful olive grove; highly recommended.

CASA DEL LAGO
Lungarno Vespucci 58
Phone: 055-216141
Double: 65,000 lire

CONSIGLI
Lungarno Vespucci 50
Phone: 055-214172
Double: 65,000 lire

CROCINI
Corso Italia 28
Phone: 055-212905
Double: 65,000 lire

Camp Sites

ITALIANI E STRANIERI
Viale Michelangelo 80
Phone: 055-6811977
320 tent sites
Closed November–March.

VILLA CAMERATA
Viale A.Righi 2-4
Phone: 055-610300
55 tent sites

Youth Hostels

VILLA CAMERATA
Viale A.Righi 2-4
Phone: 055-601451
63 rooms, April–September.
Beautiful 19th-century villa.

SANTA MONICA

Via Santa Monica 6
Phone: 055-268338
13 rooms, 111 beds.

HEALTH & EMERGENCIES

SOS: Emergency Numbers
Police: 113
Fire department: 115
Rescue Service: 215555/212222
Pharmacies/Information: 192
Auto breakdown service: 116

24-hour Drugstores and Hospitals:

COMUNALE No 13
Interno Stazione S Maria Novella
Phone: 055-263435

MOLTENI
Via Calzaiuoli 7r
Phone: 055-263490

TAVERNA
Piazza S Giovanni 20r
Phone: 055-211343

OSPEDALE DI S MARIA NUOVA
Piazza S Maria Nuova 1
Phone: 055-27581

CARECCI
Viale Morgagni 85
Phone: 055-4277111

INSTITUTO ORTOPEDICO TOSCANO
PIERO PALAGI
Viale Michelangelo 41
Phone: 055-6813811/27691

OSPEDALE OFTALMICO
Via Masaccio 213
Phone: 055-578444

PEDIATRICO MEYER
Via Luca Giordano 14
Phone: 055-4277111

BUSINESS HOURS & HOLIDAYS

Shops are open in summer: 9am–1pm, 4–8pm; in winter: 9am–1pm, 3.30–7.30pm. All grocery stores are closed Wednesday afternoon.

Holidays

New Year's Day:	1 January
Epiphany:	6 January
Shrove Tuesday	
Good Friday	
Easter Monday	
Liberation Day:	25 April
May Day:	1 May
Ascension Day	
Whit Monday	
Corpus Christi	
Proclamation of the Republic:	2 June
Assumption of the Virgin Mary (Ferragosto):	15 August
All Saints' Day:	1 November
Italian Union Day:	4 November
Festa della Madonna:	8 December
Christmas Day:	25 December
Boxing Day:	26 December

COMMUNICATIONS & MEDIA

Post and Telephone
Hours of Business: 8.15am–2.40pm; Saturday 8.15–noon; closed Sunday and holidays.
Main Office: Palazzo delle Poste
Via Pelliceria. 8.15am–1pm; Saturday 8.15am–noon. Long-distance calls around the clock.

To dial other countries first dial the international access code 00, then the country code: Australia (61); France (33); Germany (49); Japan (81); Netherlands (31); Spain (34); UK (44); US and Canada (1). If using a US credit phone card, dial the company's access number below – Sprint, Tel: 172 1877; AT&T, Tel: 172 1011; MCI, Tel: 172 1022.

Radio and Television

Raiuno, Raidue and *Raitre* are the state-run stations—the difference being that the first is allied to the Christian Democrats, the second to the Socialists and the third to the Communist Party of Italy.

Other important stations are *Canale 5, Rete 4* and *Italia 1*—all owned by Silvio Berlusconi. By now probably the second wealthiest man in Italy (after Gianni Agnelli), he is in the process of expanding his media power beyond the borders of Italy.

The real Tuscan stations are: *Teleregione, Tele Libera Firenze, Rete A, REte Mia, Canale 10,* and *Video Firenze.* Each one worse than the last. *Radio Montebeni* (108FM) plays only classical music. The most listened-to radio stations are: *Lady Radio, Radio Cuore* and *Crudelia*—and the names speak for themselves! Good political stations are: *Radio Centofiori* and *Controradio.*

Newspapers

The newsstands carry the following: *La Nazione, La Repubblica, Il Tirreno, L'Unita', Firenze La Sera, Firenze Spettacolo* and *La Pulce.*

The Tuscan newspaper per se is the conservative *La Nazione.* The more progressive *La Repubblica* is actually a nationally circulated newspaper with a detailed local supplement. *Il Tirreno* is distributed mainly along the coast. *Firenze La Sera* and *Firenze Spettacolo* provide information about events and local affairs, while *La Pulce,* the 'Flea', is full of classified ads.

CALENDAR OF EVENTS

JANUARY: Pitti Uomo, Pitti Bimbo—Fashion Week
FEBRUARY: Florence Gift Mart (also in September)
FEBRUARY/MARCH: Carnival
MARCH: Diplo, Art Book Fair

APRIL/MAY: Arts and Crafts Fair
MAY/JUNE: Maggio Musicale Fiorentino, opera, ballet and concerts. For premieres reserve well in advance.
24 and 28 JUNE: Calcio in Costume, football game in mediaeval costumes.
24 JUNE: S Giovanni, the patron saint of Florence; fireworks. One of the most important public festivals.
7 SEPTEMBER: *Rificolona:* lantern procession.
SEPTEMBER/OCTOBER: Biennale dell' Antiquariato in the Palazzo Strozzi. Most important antiques event.
NOVEMBER: Borsa del Turismo Congressuale: covers everything concerning the tourist and convention trade.
DECEMBER: Festival dei Popoli

NIGHTLIFE

Florence is not New York, and there is not that much of a disco scene—especially since most places close quite early. During the last few years there has been as much quarrelling over closing times as over the pedestrian precinct. Many discos are outside town, because concessions are no longer issued for the city centre (unless, of course, you belong to the right party).

Discotheques

LA CAPITALE
Via del Fosso Macinante 2–4
Phone: 055-356723

Outdoor discotheque; plenty of room. Best 'hunting ground'. Opens at 10pm.

MANILA
Piazza Matteucci
Campi Bisenzio
Phone: 055-894121
Live music; guests include members of the fashion trade, the art world and avant garde circles. Opens at 10pm.

FANDANGO
Via dell'Erta Canina 12
Phone: 055-2343903
Opens at 10pm. You can shake a leg downstairs and then sit for a drink upstairs. Predominantly young.

JACKIE O
Via dell'Erta Canina 24b
Phone: 055-216146

Posh disco for those who have made it to the top.

ROCKCAFÉ
Borgo degli Albizi 66r
Phone: 055-244662
Opens at 10pm. The only rock disco in town. Also live concerts.

YAB YUM
Via Sassetti 5r
Phone: 055-282018
Opens at 11pm. Right downtown. Droves of in-crowders.

TENAX
Via Pratese 47
Phone: 055-37050
Opens at 10pm. Multimedia meeting place of the artistic and musical avant-garde.

SPACE ELECTRONIC
Via Palazzuolo 37
Phone: 055-293082
Opens at 9.30 p.m. Largest disco in Florence with special effects, lasers, spaceships, videos, etc.

MARAMAO
Via de' Macci 79r
Opens at 12pm. Closed on Sunday and Monday. The city's newest acquisition.

Bars
There are numerous bars. Here is a selection of the most distinctive.

CAFFÉ
Piazza Pitti 9
Phone: 055-296241
Closed Monday. Exclusive; furnished with antiques, sofas just like in Grandma's parlour—ideal for a quiet evening.

LA DOLCE VITA
Piazza del Carmine
Phone: 055-284595;
10pm–1am; closed Sunday.
In summer this is one of the most heavily frequented bars in Florence. Very 'in' among those who want to be seen. If you cannot get in—which is usually the case—you take a seat on the roof of a parked car to enjoy the beautiful setting of the Piazza.

ROSE'S
Via del Parione 26r
Phone: 055-287090
Closed Sunday.
Always full. Plenty of cocktails and long drinks.

CAFFÉ CIBREO
Via del Verrocchio 5r
Phone: 055-2345853
8pm–1am.
Closed Sunday and Monday.
Quiet and refined. Very sophisticated.

CAFÉ VOLTAIRE
Via della Scala 9r
Phone: 055-218255
8am–4pm; Sunday 5pm–4am.
Frequently interesting programmes.
Former Sixties crowd watering hole.
Now a private club: membership required.

BOCCASCENA
Viale Europa 49-51
Phone: 055-685996
Closed Monday.
Parking is no problem here! The only reason for its popularity? Occasional celebrity visitors and live music.

ART BAR
Via del Moro
Very small—extremely popular among foreign students.

MONTECARLA CLUB
Via dei Bardi 2
Phone: 055-2340259
Amusing kitsch.

Downtown Bars and Clubs

PASZKOWSKI
Piazza della Repubblica 6
Phone: 055-210236
Closed Monday.
An institution. Open until 1.30am. Evergreens on the piano. Elderly ladies have a great time here.

GILLI
Piazza della Repubblica 39r
Phone: 055-296310
Closed Tuesday. Sit and watch the people stroll by . . . preferably in the first spring sunshine.

GIACOSA
Via Tornabuoni 83r
Phone: 055-296226
Closed Sunday. At noon the businessmen and lawyers meet for a hasty bite to eat.

RIVOIRE
Piazza della Signoria 5r
Phone: 055-214412
Closed Monday, as well as the second half of January. Sitting in the sun,

taking in the Piazza—if there is no construction work going on! Otherwise you cannot say you have been to Florence.

GIUBBE ROSSE
Piazza della Repubblica 13r
Phone: 055-212280
Closed Thursday.
Historical bar—once the haunt of artists and intellectuals.

PROCACCI
Via Tornabuoni 64r
Phone: 055-211656
Same hours of business as the shops. A truffle sandwich is simply *bon ton*!

ROBIGLIO
Via dei Serevi 112 r
Phone: 055-214501
Via Tosinghi 11r
Phone: 055-215013
Closed Monday. Good coffee shop.

CAFFELLATTE
Via degli Alfani 93r
Phone: 055-2478878
8am–1.30pm, 3.30–7.30pm.
Closed Sunday. If a *cappuccino con brioche* is not enough, this is the right address. Warm rolls, cakes, granola, tea in all variations, etc.

Live Music

CHIODO FISSO
Via Alighieri 16r
Phone: 055-2381290
Owner and bard in one person.

JAZZ CLUB
Via Nuova dei Caccini 3
Phone: 055-2479700
The oldest jazz joint in town. Beer.

RIFLISSI D'EPOCA
Via dei Renai 13r
Opens at 10pm and has the longest hours. Continuous turnover: the audience changes as the night progresses.

SPAZIO 1
Via del Sole
Belongs to the art house cinema of the same name. Meeting place for intellectual youngsters.

Museums

PITTI PALACE
Appartamenti Monumentali—Piazza Pitti
Phone: 055-210323

MEDICI CHAPEL
Piazza Madonna degli Aldobrandini
9am–2pm, Sunday and holidays: 9am–1pm, closed Monday.
Phone: 055-213206
Admission: 4,350 lire

CENACOLO DEL GHIRLANDAIO
Borgo Ognissanti 42
Tuesday, Thursday and Saturday: 9am–noon, closed Sunday and holidays.
Phone: 055-296802
Free admission.

CHIOSTRO DELLO SCALZO
Via Cavour 69
9am–2pm; holidays 9am–1pm, closed Monday.
Phone: 055-472812
Free admission.

COLLEZIONE CONTI-BENACOSSI
Giardino di Boboli
Piazza Pitti
Upon request: c/o Segretaria degli Uffizi
Phone: 055-218341

CROCIFISSIONE DEL PERUGINO
Borgo Pinti 58
9–noon, 5–7pm.
Phone: 055-2478420

GALLERIA DELL'ACCADEMIA
Via Ricasoli 60
9am–2pm; Sunday and holidays 9am–1pm; closed Monday.
Phone: 055-214375
Admission: 4,000 lire

GALLERIA D'ARTE MODERNA
Piazza Pitti-Palazzo Pitti
9am–2pm; Sunday and holidays 9am–
1pm; closed Monday.
Phone: 055-287096
Admission: 4,000 lire

GALLERIA DEL COSTUME
Giardino di Boboli-Piazza Pitti
9am–2pm; Sunday and holidays: 9am–
1pm; closed Monday.
Phone: 055-212557
Admission: 3,000 lire

GALLERIA PALATINA
Piazza Pitti-Palazzo Pitti
9am–2pm; Sunday and holidays: 9am–
1pm; closed Monday.
Phone: 055-210323
Admission: 3,000 lire

GALLERIA DEGLI UFFIZI
Loggiato degli Uffizi 6
9am–7pm; Sunday and holidays: 9am–
1pm; closed Monday.
Phone: 055-218341
Admission: 5,000 lire

GIARDINO DI BOBOLI
Piazza Pitti
Phone: 055-213440. Free admission.

MUSEO ARCHEOLOGICO
Via della Colonna 36
9am–2pm; Sunday and holidays: 9am–
1pm; closed Monday.
Phone: 055-2478641
Admission: 3,000 lire

MUSEO DEGLI ARGENTI
Piazza Pitti-Palazzo Pitti
9am–2pm; Sunday and holidays 9am–
1pm; closed Monday.
Phone: 055-212557
Admission: 3,000 lire

MUSEO DELLA CASA FIORENTINA ANTICA
Via Porta Rossa 13
9am–2pm; Sunday and holidays: 8am–
1pm.

Phone: 055-216518
Admission: 2,000 lire

MUSEO NAZIONALE DEL BARGELLO
Via del Proconsolo 4
9am–2pm; Sunday and holidays: 9am–
1pm, closed Mondays.
Phone: 055-210801
Admission: 3,000 lire

MUSEO DELLE PORCELLANE
Palazzo Pitti
9am–2pm; Sunday and holidays: 9am–
1pm, closed Monday.
Phone: 055-212557
Admission: 3,000 lire

MUSEO DI SAN MARCO
Piazza San Marco 1
9am–2pm; Sunday and holidays: 9am–
1pm, closed Monday.
Phone: 055-210741
Admission: 3,000 lire

MUSEO STORICO TOPOGRAFICO 'FIRENZE COM'ERA'
Via dell'Oriuolo 24
9am–2pm; Sunday and holidays: 8am–
1pm, closed Thursday.
Phone: 055-298483
Admission: 2,000 lire

GALLERIA DELLO SPEDALE DEGLI INNOCENTI
Piazza SS Annunziata 12
9am–2pm; Sunday and holidays: 8am–1pm, closed Wednesday.
Phone: 055-243670
Admission: 3,000 lire

MUSEO S MARIA NOVELLA
Piazza S Maria Novella
9am–2pm; Sunday and holidays: 8am–1pm, closed Friday.
Phone: 055-282187
Admission: 3,000 lire

PALAZZO VECCHIO E QUARTIERI MONUMENTALI
Piazza della Signoria
9am–7pm; Sunday and holidays: 8am–1pm.
Phone: 055-2768465
Admission: 4,000 lire

MUSEO DI STORIA DELLA SCIENZA
Piazza de'Giudici 1
Monday–Saturday 9.30am–1pm; Monday, Wednesday and Friday: also 2–5pm; closed Sunday and holidays.
Phone: 055-293493
Admission: 5,000 lire

MUSEO ZOOLOGICO 'LA SPECOLA'
Via Romana 17
Monday, Tuesday, Thursday, Friday and Saturday: 9am–noon.
Phone: 055-222451
Free admission.

ORTO BOTANICO 'GIARDINO DEI SEMPLICI'
Via Micheli 3
Monday, Wednesday, and Friday: 9–12am. Phone: 055-284696
Free admission.

Theatre

TEATRO COMUNALE
Corso Italia 12
Phone: 055-27791

TEATRO DELLA PERGOLA
Via della Pergola 12-32
Phone: 055-2479651

NICCOLINI
Via Ricasoli 5
Phone: 055-2398333

VERDI
Via Ghibellina 99
Phone: 055-2396242

Ticket Sales

BOX OFFICE
Via della Pergola 10a/r
Phone: 055-243361

SPORT

Golf
GOLF DELL'UGOLINO
Via Chiantigiana 3
Impruneta
Phone: 055-2051155

Athletics, Roller Skating, Tennis
ASSOCIAZIONE SPORTIVA ASSI
Viale Michelangelo 64
Phone: 055-6812686

Rowing
SOCIETA' CANOTTIERI 'FIRENZE'
Lungarno de'Medici 8
Phone: 055-282130

Riding
CENTRO IPPICO TOSCANO 'LE CASCINE'
Via Vespucci 5a
Phone: 055-372621

Boxing
BOXING CLUB
Via G da Montorsoli
Phone: 055-714528

Table-tennis
Viale Mille 11
Phone: 055-575716

Fencing
CIRCOLO SCHERMA FIRENZE
Via Fiume 5
Phone: 055-282250

USEFUL ADDRESSES

Banks

BANCA C STEINHAUSLIN & C
Via dei Sassetti 4
Phone: 055-27621

BANCA NAZIONALE DEL LAVORO
Via Strozzi 1
Phone: 055-27931

BANCA TOSCANA
Via Panclado 4
Phone: 055-4361510

BANCA MERCANTILE ITALIANA
Piazza Davanzati 3
Phone: 055-27651

BANCA FEDERICO DEL VECCHIO
Via dei Banchi 5
Phone: 055-288402

CREDITO ITALIANO
Via Veccietti 11

Phone: 055-27971

CASSA DI RISPARMIO DI FIRENZE
Via Bufalini 4
Phone: 055-27801

BANCA COMMERCIALE ITALIANA
Via Strozzi 8
Phone: 055-27851

Airlines

AIR FRANCE
Borgo SS Apostoli 9
Phone: 055-218335

ALITALIA
Lungarno Acciaioli 10-12r
Phone: 055-27888

BRITISH AIRWAYS
Via Vigna Nuova 36r
Phone: 055-218655

IBERIA
Piazza Antinori 2
Phone: 055-215227

KLM ROYAL DUTCH AIRWAYS
Piazza Antinori 2
Phone: 055-284043

LUFTHANSA
Via Pellicceria 6
Phone: 055-2382890

OLYMPIC AIRWAYS
Via Por Santa Maria 4
Phone: 055-282338

SAS SCANDINAVIAN AIRLINES
Lungarno Acciaioli 8
Phone: 055-2382701

SWISSAIR
Via Parione 1
Phone: 055-295051

THAI
Via dei Conti 4. Phone: 055-294372

TWA
Piazza Santa Trinita 1r
Phone: 055-2382795

Travel Agencies

AIRLINES BOOKING CENTER
Via dei Banchi 23-27r
Phone: 055-473493

AMERICAN EXPRESS COMPANY
Via Guicciardini 49r
Phone: 055-278751

CIT (COMPAGNIA ITALIANA TURISMO)
Via Cavour 54r
Phone: 055-294306
Piazza Stazione 51r
Phone: 055-284145

EYRE & HUMBERT
Via del Parione 56r
Phone: 055-262251

INTERTRAVEL
Via Lamberti 39-41r
Phone: 055-217936

WAGON-LITS TURISMO
Via del Giglio 27r
Phone: 055-218851

USEFUL INFORMATION

Tourist Information
The printed *Pagine Gialle per il Turismo* contain a convenient compilation of addresses and telephone numbers of institutions which are of particular interest to tourists. Either *Pro Loco* or the *Azienda Autonoma del Turismo* have offices in all major towns in Tuscany—but they are hardly helpful. Usually they are closed or they have run out of information material. On the other hand, you do sometimes meet some very nice and helpful people there.

Lost & Found

OGGETTI SMARRITI
Via Circondarioa 19
Phone: 055-367943

PARCO AUTO REQUISITE
(Parking lot for towed-away cars)
Via Circondaria 19
Phone: 055-351562

Thermal Baths

TERME DI FIRENZE
Fasciani-Impruneta (Firenze)
Cia Cassia 193
April–October

TERME DI BAGNOLO
Monterotondo Marittimo (Grosseto)
Phone: 0566-96633

TERME DIE PETRIOLO
Petriolo (Grosseto)
Phone: 0564-908871
1 April–7 January

TERME S GIOVANNI
Saline-Porto Ferraio (Livorno)
Phone: 0565-92680
20 April–31 October

TERME VALLE DEL SOLE
Via Aurelia Nord
Venturina-Caldana Terme
(Livorno)
Phone: 0586-51066
April–November

TERME DI BAGNI DI LUCCA
Bagni di Lucca (Lucca)
Phone: 0583-87223
March–November

TERME DIE CASCIANA
Piazza Garibaldi 9
Casciana Terme (Pisa)
Phone: 0587-646112
1 Apri–30 November

TERME DIE S GUILIANO
Piazza Repubblica
S Guiliano Terme (Pisa)
Phone: 050-818047

TERME DI MONSUMMANO
Monsummano Terme (Pistoia)
Grotta Giusti
Phone: 0572-51008
1 April–20 November (Grotta Giusti)
16 May–20 October (Grotta Parlanti)

TERME DIE MONTECATINI
Viale Verdi 41
Montecatini Terme (Pistoia)
Phone: 0572-75851

TERME DI CHIANCIANO
Viale Roma
Chianciano Terme (Siena)
Phone: 0578-63037
16 April–15 November

TERME DI MONTEPULCIANO
Via delle Terme 46
Terme di Montepulciano (Siena)
Phone: 0578-79086
16 April–31 October

TERME DIE RAPOLANO
Rapolano Terme (Siena)
Phone: 0577-724030
June–20 October

TERME DI S FILIPPO
Bagni di S Filippo (Siena)
Phone: 0577-872982
1 June–15 October

Children and Youth Activities

The Cooperativa dei Ragazzi (Via San
Gallo 27, Phone: 055-287500) has
plenty of books (also in English and
French) and games for children of all
ages. The staff are also glad to pass
on information. Sometimes there are
performances in the afternoon.

LUDOTECA CENTRALE
(Piazza SS Annunziata 13)
Phone for information: 055-2478386.

BABY-SITTING
Via del Castellaccio 45r
Phone: 055-289382

**CHILDREN'S THEATRE
INFORMATION/BOX OFFICE**
Via della Pergola 10
Phone: 055-243361

49, 50, 51, 52, 53, 57, 58, 59, 60, 61	**Silvia Brunelli**
62, 65ᴛ, 69, 72ᴛ, 73, 75, 76, 89, 90, 92	
100, 101	**Edizioni Ciao**
99	**Edizioni Novanta**
5, 20, 22ᴛ, 24ʙ, 25, 30, 31, 33, 38, 39ʙ, 40,	**Stefano Geraldi**
41, 42, 43, 45, 46, 68, 71, 72ʙ, 74, 77, 78,	
82, 86, 98, 104, 105, 106, 112–13	
3, 54, 55, 63, 79, 87, 91, 107ʙ,	**Hans Jürgen Truöl**
109, 110, 112, 115, 116, 123	
21, 22ʙ, 23, 24ᴛ, 27, 28, 29, 34, 35, 37, 39ᴛ, 47, 65ʙ,	**Bill Wassman**
66, 67, 81, 83, 84, 85, 94, 95, 97, 103, 107ᴛ, 111	
Cover Design	**Klaus Geisler**
Cartography	**Berndtson & Berndtson**

NOTES

INSIGHT GUIDES

COLORSET NUMBERS

You'll find the colorset number on the spine of each Insight Guide.

INSIGHT *POCKET* GUIDES

. . . .
United States: Houghton Mifflin Company, Boston MA 02108
Tel: (800) 2253362 Fax: (800) 4589501

Canada: Thomas Allen & Son, 390 Steelcase Road East
Markham, Ontario L3R 1G2
Tel: (416) 4759126 Fax: (416) 4756747

Great Britain: GeoCenter UK, Hampshire RG22 4BJ
Tel: (256) 817987 Fax: (256) 817988

Worldwide: Höfer Communications Singapore 2262
Tel: (65) 8612755 Fax: (65) 8616438

" I was first drawn to the Insight Guides by the excellent "Nepal" volume. I can think of no book which so effectively captures the essence of a country. Out of these pages leaped the Nepal I know – the captivating charm of a people and their culture. I've since discovered and enjoyed the entire Insight Guide Series. Each volume deals with a country or city in the same sensitive depth, which is nowhere more evident than in the superb photography. "

Sir Edmund Hillary

NOTES